Tax Smart

Tax Smart

A Beginner's Guide to Keeping More of What You Earn

Nicolette Sharma

Mindful Pages

Published in 2026

ISBN: 9789374121221 (PB)
ISBN: 9789374124321 (eBook)

Published by

Mindful Pages
Imprint of Alpha Editions LLC
312 W. 2nd St #1834
Casper, WY 82601, USA

This book was developed using advanced writing tools to support the drafting and ideation process. All content has been thoughtfully curated, refined, and reviewed to ensure quality and relevance.

Content

Introduction

Tax Smart: A Beginner's Guide to Keeping More of What You Earn

A peculiar irony lurks in the lives of many first-time founders and self-employed professionals. They can quote their product's price to the nearest penny, negotiate supplier terms with forensic precision, and project cash flows with a confidence bordering on bravado—yet when it comes to taxes, their guesses are seasonal at best. Ask when the next payment is due, and you may hear "sometime in April" or "whenever the accountant says so." This dissonance—mathematical clarity in commerce, foggy vagueness in taxation—is more than an amusing quirk. It is the root of unnecessary penalties, sleepless nights, and the persistent fear that one is always about to fall foul of a rule written in a distant ledger.

Tax, in other words, is often treated as an ambush. Not an orderly civic duty, but a sudden strike that arrives months after decisions are made. The very delay built into tax systems—earn now, pay later—creates a psychological trap. People respond well to immediate consequences; they are less adept when costs arrive six or twelve months after the act. The invoice that seemed profitable in June becomes the reason cash runs dry in January. The new laptop, once a thrilling investment, becomes a point of confusion: was it an expense, or must it be spread across years? Out of this fog emerges panic: a sense that tax is unknowable, hostile, and always one step away from catching you out.

This book is written to dispel that fog. Its promise is not flamboyant riches or clever tricks, but something quieter and ultimately more valuable: predictability. By adopting a simple framework—*Money In, Money Out, Right Time*—you can transform tax from a yearly ambush into a weekly rhythm. With a half-hour ritual each week, founders can keep pace with their obligations, tame the paperwork beast before it grows fangs, and price their work with the confidence that what remains after tax is truly theirs. The aim is modest: fewer shocks, cleaner cash flow, and more of your hard-earned income preserved. But modest gains, repeated week by week, are what separate those who endure from those who burn out.

The Old Fear

To appreciate why such a modest promise matters, it helps to see how unusual our moment is. Tax anxiety is not new. In medieval England, peasants often had a better grasp of their obligations—tithes, manorial dues, the king's levy—than today's sole traders have of VAT or quarterly instalments. Their dues were brutal, but they were visible. A man could stand in the field and know that every tenth sheaf would be carted away at harvest. There was no illusion of surprise. Modern tax systems, by contrast, are intricate abstractions. The harvest is continuous, the levies deferred, and the language so technical that even educated professionals stumble. The result is a peculiar alienation: we know we must pay, yet we do not know how to calculate or anticipate with ease.

The 20th century only deepened this distance. Withholding taxes on wages trained millions to see tax as a silent deduction, invisible until year-end reconciliations. For employees, this opacity may be tolerable. For founders, it is ruinous. Unlike salaries, self-employed earnings are raw and untamed: gross receipts that must be trimmed by expenses, filtered through local laws, and staggered across payment dates. To misjudge is not to lose a little, but sometimes to lose the business.

A Portable System

What makes matters worse is the overwhelming noise surrounding taxation. New founders are often greeted by encyclopaedic tomes—dense with jargon, footnotes, and labyrinthine exceptions—when all they seek is clarity on whether to invoice today or next week. This book resists that impulse. Instead of drowning you in detail, it offers a portable system, designed to travel across borders. Its skeleton is universal: income must be counted when it arrives, expenses must be ordinary and necessary, and timing must align with rules that repeat more than they deviate. Around this skeleton hang the regional quirks—the U.S. Schedule C, the U.K. Self Assessment, Canada's T2125, India's ITR forms. These will be acknowledged in sidebars, without hijacking the narrative.

This global framing is not an affectation. It reflects the reality of modern entrepreneurship, where a designer in London may invoice a client in Toronto through a U.S. platform, and a coder in Bangalore may sell digital products to a customer in Berlin. The boundaries of jurisdiction remain stubbornly local, but the commerce of individuals is irreversibly global. What founders need, therefore, is not a textbook for each country but a way of thinking that survives the crossing of borders.

The Tuesday Test

The litmus test of this book is not theoretical rigour but practical relevance. Tax-smart behaviour must prove itself on a Tuesday afternoon, when decisions are made in real time. Do you send the invoice before month's end, or wait? Do you buy the laptop now, or next quarter? Do you pay yourself a salary, a dividend, or simply draw the cash? These are the hinge-points where profit turns into liability—or into resilience. They cannot be postponed until a future meeting with an accountant. They cannot be left to rules remembered vaguely from last year's filing. They demand clarity in the moment.

Every chapter in this book is written with that demand in mind. Concepts are pared back to their essence, examples are drawn from the dilemmas founders actually face, and rituals are proposed to anchor each insight into habit. The aim is not encyclopaedic mastery, but durable fluency: the ability to act with confidence, not guesswork.

What Is at Stake

Why does this matter? At one level, the stakes are obvious: money. Every pound or dollar unnecessarily lost to penalties or poor planning is money not available for reinvestment, growth, or personal security. But at another level, the stakes are psychological. Tax confusion corrodes confidence. It encourages avoidance, which in turn breeds more confusion. Many founders will recognise the vicious cycle: paperwork postponed until guilt sets in, frantic sorting before a deadline, and a vague vow to "do better next year." This cycle wastes not only cash but emotional energy. It makes entrepreneurship feel precarious even when the underlying business is sound.

The preventative playbook offered here is an attempt to replace that cycle with a steadier rhythm. The weekly ritual is the spine of this rhythm. Capture income, classify expenses, set aside tax, glance at the calendar—thirty minutes, no more. This discipline, once embedded, reframes the founder's relationship with tax. It becomes less a threat from outside, more a managed cost of doing business, like rent or utilities. In this reframe lies freedom: the freedom to focus on work without the background hum of dread.

A Motif: The Set-Aside Jar

To ground this reframe, consider a simple image: the jar on the shelf. In many households, there was once a jar where coins were dropped for future obligations—a child's school trip, a family holiday, an emergency. It was not sophisticated, but it was reliable. Every contribution reduced the future burden. Modern founders need their own jar—not a literal glass vessel, but a dedicated account or ledger entry where tax money is placed aside each week. The jar becomes a motif throughout this book: a symbol of foresight, of discipline made visible. It embodies the principle that what feels abstract becomes manageable when materialised.

Looking Ahead

As you move through these chapters, you will encounter decisions about structure—whether to remain a sole trader or form a company; about income—what counts, and when; about transaction taxes—what you collect at the till and why it is never truly yours; about deductions—where the line between legitimate and reckless lies. You will learn how to treat home offices and vehicles without inviting grief, how to anticipate quarterly payments without panic, how to keep records that think for you, how to work with accountants wisely, how to approach audits without fear, and how to transform year-end from a mad scramble into a planned close. The arc culminates in something rare: not a temporary fix, but a personal tax policy that you write for yourself, a set of rules you can live by.

The questions animating this book are deceptively simple. What does it take to be both compliant and confident? How can a founder make tax part of their operating rhythm rather than a seasonal shock? What habits separate those who lurch from crisis to crisis from those who steadily accumulate wealth? These questions matter not just for individuals, but for the society that depends on their enterprise. A culture of compliance built on clarity is more resilient than one built on confusion and punishment.

The Invitation

This, then, is your invitation: to replace panic with policy, dread with rhythm, and guesswork with clarity. The path is not glamorous. It does not promise loopholes or clever tricks. What it offers is sturdier: a preventative playbook that makes tax ordinary, knowable, and endurable. If you follow the system—Money In, Money Out, Right Time—you will discover that tax is not the enemy of entrepreneurship, but a predictable partner in its discipline. And in that predictability lies the reward every founder seeks: to keep more of what you earn, with fewer surprises along the way.

Chapter 1
The Founder's Tax Gap

On a damp Tuesday in November, a freelance designer sits in a café, laptop open, coffee cooling beside her. She knows she should be sorting receipts, or at least logging last week's invoices. Instead, she scrolls through her inbox, searching for distraction. The figures in her head are rough guesses: she believes she earned enough this quarter to be "comfortable," but has no idea what portion of that income is already spoken for by the tax office. She promises herself she will deal with it next week—only next week will look remarkably similar to this one. Months later, an unexpected demand arrives. Panic sets in. She is hardly alone.

This paralysis is not caused by ignorance. Our designer is intelligent, organised, even meticulous in her craft. Yet when it comes to tax, the confidence evaporates. The irony is striking: the same mind that can calculate client pricing to the penny cannot summon the will to estimate a quarterly payment. This is the founder's tax gap—the space between intellectual ability and actual behaviour when facing obligations that are both abstract and delayed. It is not a failing of character, but a predictable response to how human psychology collides with fiscal systems.

At the heart of this collision are two well-documented biases: *loss aversion* and *ambiguity aversion*. We feel losses more acutely than equivalent gains, and we recoil from decisions where outcomes are uncertain. Taxes trigger both. To part with money today for an obligation months away feels like a guaranteed loss; to project future liability feels riddled with ambiguity. Faced with this unpleasant cocktail, many founders do what humans often do—avoid. They ignore estimated payments, postpone bookkeeping, or convince themselves that clarity can wait. But avoidance has its own cost. When the reckoning comes, it feels doubly unfair: a punishment delayed until the guilt has faded, a financial blow disconnected from the moment that caused it.

Naming this pattern matters. It reframes panic not as incompetence but as a design flaw in the system. Once recognised, it can be addressed. Instead of seeing tax dread as a moral weakness—"I'm bad with numbers, I'm disorganised"—the founder can see it as a gap to be closed with structure and habit. That shift, from shame to strategy, is the first step toward mastery.

If panic is the problem, what provides stability? Not esoteric loopholes or dazzling tricks, but three levers available to every founder: structure, records, and timing. These are deceptively ordinary, yet together they account for most tax outcomes. Structure is the legal form you choose—sole trader, partnership, company—and the channels through which money flows. Records are the quality of your bookkeeping, from receipts captured to expenses categorised. Timing is the discipline of aligning action with calendars, whether that means billing at the right moment or making payments before deadlines.

Consider the analogy of a modest garden. You may not have rare seeds or elaborate tools, but if you plant in season, water consistently, and keep the soil healthy, the yield is reliable. Tax discipline works the same way. Average decisions, applied steadily across these three levers, outperform sporadic brilliance. The founder who keeps plain but consistent records will fare better than the one who masters advanced strategies yet neglects paperwork for months at a time. What matters is repeatability. This book, and this chapter in particular, promise repeatable moves—not secret tricks.

Still, even with clear levers, a second challenge arises: the sheer diversity of tax systems. A founder in California files a Schedule C; her counterpart in London completes a Self Assessment; in Toronto it is the T2125; in Mumbai, an ITR form. Each carries its own language, quirks, and thresholds. For the novice, the array is overwhelming.

But beneath the local labels lie country-agnostic rules. Income is taxable when earned or received. Expenses must be ordinary, necessary, and demonstrable. Capital assets are treated differently from consumables. These principles travel. The founder who grasps them can operate across borders with confidence, checking local quirks only when necessary. This balance is crucial: to drown in exceptions is paralysing, but to ignore them entirely is reckless. What follows in this book is a discipline of separation—general rules in the main text, jurisdiction notes in sidebars for the United States, the United Kingdom, Canada, and India. The effect is clarity without overload, universality without naïveté.

Yet rules and levers alone do not cure panic. What transforms theory into resilience is ritual. Tax becomes manageable when it is not an annual event but a weekly habit. Picture this: thirty minutes each week, no more. Capture income. Classify expenses. Update the tax set-aside. Scan a short calendar. That is all. A modest cadence, repeated, that prevents the quarter-end scramble and the year-end dread.

The simplicity of the ritual is deceptive. Over time, it shapes decisions in the moment. Knowing you will log the week's activity soon discourages delay. Seeing the tax jar fill each week reframes obligations as manageable increments rather than sudden shocks. The ritual becomes the thread running through the founder's financial life—anchoring tactics, stabilising confidence, and steadily closing the gap between panic and fluency.

This chapter, then, is about exposure and repair. It exposes the hidden forces—psychological biases, structural levers, jurisdictional quirks—that widen the tax gap. And it sketches the beginnings of repair, pointing toward a rhythm that transforms avoidance into confidence. The pages ahead will not erase complexity; they will make it navigable. They will not remove responsibility; they will make it bearable.

So as you turn into the chapter proper, ask yourself: what would it mean if tax no longer provoked panic but provided clarity? What if, instead of fearing the delayed blow, you could predict its weight, set aside its cost, and proceed with your work unhindered? These questions are not abstract. They are the difference between a founder who stumbles from fine to fine, and one who builds a business on stable ground. This chapter begins the shift. It names the gap—and shows how to cross it.

Why Smart People Panic About Tax

It is one of the strangest contradictions of modern professional life: the very people capable of solving complex equations, managing high-stakes negotiations, or designing systems of exquisite precision will flinch, freeze, or procrastinate when faced with their own taxes. The paradox is everywhere. A software engineer who can debug thousands of lines of code shies away from logging expenses. A consultant who can calculate margins to the decimal postpones an estimated payment until the penalties arrive. These are not isolated quirks; they are part of a pattern, one rooted not in intelligence or diligence, but in the peculiar way human psychology collides with delayed financial obligations.

Tax anxiety does not discriminate. It grips the ambitious start-up founder, the meticulous freelancer, and the seasoned professional alike. What unites them is not a lack of capacity, but the experience of making decisions today whose consequences materialise only months, or even years, later. We are wired for immediacy; our brains excel at reacting to the present. Taxes, however, belong to the future. That disjunction—between action and delayed effect—creates fertile ground for fear, avoidance, and poor decision-making.

At the core of this lies *loss aversion.* Decades of behavioural economics research, from Daniel Kahneman and Amos Tversky onwards, has shown that humans feel the sting of loss roughly twice as intensely as they feel the pleasure of an equivalent gain. To hand over money now, whether to a tax authority or to a savings account earmarked for tax, feels like a palpable loss. The gain—avoiding a penalty months later—is too abstract, too remote to carry emotional weight. This is why setting aside a portion of income for future liabilities feels painful in the moment, even though intellectually we know it is necessary.

But loss aversion is only half the story. Taxes also embody *ambiguity aversion.* Unlike a clear, known risk—say, the roll of a die with fixed odds—ambiguity presents unknown probabilities. Founders are asked to project income, estimate liabilities, and navigate rules they only half understand. The probabilities are not merely uncertain; they are often unknowable without expertise. Faced with such ambiguity, many retreat into inaction. They postpone bookkeeping, reasoning that clarity will come later. They skip estimated payments, hoping that cash flow today is a better bet than gambling on uncertain liabilities. Ambiguity paralyses not because the decisions are impossible, but because they are clouded in uncertainty, and uncertainty is deeply uncomfortable.

The effects of these twin aversions ripple through everyday business life. Consider quarterly estimated payments. A founder knows they should set money aside and send it to the tax authority. But the numbers are fuzzy. How much did they really earn last quarter? Were certain expenses deductible? Might revenue dip or surge in the coming months? Faced with ambiguity, the founder delays. Loss aversion then seals the hesitation: paying today feels like a definite reduction, while delaying offers the comfort of cash in hand. By the time the reckoning arrives, the liability has grown heavier, compounded by penalties, and what might have been manageable in increments becomes overwhelming in bulk.

Bookkeeping suffers a similar fate. Logging receipts, categorising expenses, or reconciling bank statements are all tasks whose benefit is delayed. The future self will appreciate the order, but the present self sees only drudgery. So the founder defers. The ambiguity of partial records builds over time, transforming a small clerical chore into a looming chaos. When the deadline finally approaches, the scramble is frantic, the quality is compromised, and the experience is once again framed as panic rather than control.

What is striking is how predictable this cycle is. It is not evidence of laziness, incompetence, or some personal shortcoming. It is the logical outcome of the way human psychology interacts with systems of delayed consequence. A tax code designed to withhold money instantly, as with salaried employees, largely sidesteps this trap. But self-employed professionals and founders face it in full, because their earnings arrive undiminished and their obligations deferred. What looks like a personal flaw is, in truth, a structural mismatch between human cognition and fiscal design.

Seeing tax panic in this light is liberating. Once it is recognised as a system flaw rather than a personal failing, the founder can shift from self-reproach to prevention. The key lies not in changing human nature, but in designing habits that compensate for it. By reframing taxes as a series of small, consistent behaviours rather than a distant reckoning, the psychological barriers lose much of their power. This book proposes such habits, beginning with the simplest of all: a thirty-minute weekly ritual.

Imagine the effect of a routine so ordinary it becomes automatic. Capture the week's income. Classify the week's expenses. Transfer a fraction into a tax set-aside account. Glance at the calendar for deadlines ahead. Half an hour, no more. The ritual does not erase loss aversion, but it dilutes it: paying in small increments feels less painful than parting with a lump sum. It does not dissolve ambiguity, but it contains it: ambiguity shrinks when records are fresh and up to date. Over time, the ritual builds a rhythm that replaces dread with confidence.

This reframing also restores dignity. Too many founders experience tax as a source of shame—believing that their avoidance signals irresponsibility or incapacity. In truth, they are responding exactly as behavioural science predicts. The smarter the person, the more acute the paradox often feels: they know they *should* manage better, which makes the avoidance sting more deeply. Naming the bias breaks the loop. It allows founders to see themselves not as flawed individuals but as participants in a flawed design. And once the design is visible, it can be redesigned.

There is, however, a deeper insight at stake. Taxes reveal something universal about human behaviour: our struggle with time. We live in the present, but much of life demands that we act for the future. Saving for retirement, maintaining health, nurturing relationships—all these share the same tension between immediate sacrifice and delayed benefit. Taxes are simply the most unforgiving version of this tension, because the penalties are legal, financial, and public. To learn how to manage tax panic, then, is to learn something larger: how to live responsibly with the future always pressing against the present.

The founder's tax gap is thus both narrow and vast. Narrow, because it often comes down to missed receipts, skipped estimates, and delayed reconciliations. Vast, because it reflects the enduring human challenge of aligning today's actions with tomorrow's consequences. The ritual of prevention—small, consistent, structured—is not just a financial tool. It is a philosophical stance, an assertion that one can meet the future not with panic, but with preparation.

The question remains: if the trap is predictable and the solution modest, why do so many intelligent people still fall into it? Perhaps because the design flaw is invisible until it is named. Perhaps because avoidance offers fleeting comfort, and comfort often wins in the short term. Or perhaps because the culture of entrepreneurship celebrates risk-taking in business but rarely teaches discipline in finance. Whatever the reason, the panic persists—until a system of prevention is put in place.

And so the challenge stands. Will you continue to let loss aversion and ambiguity dictate your decisions, allowing dread to accumulate until deadlines force a crisis? Or will you reframe the problem as a structural gap, and begin to bridge it with steady, modest habits? The answer lies not in brilliance but in rhythm. And rhythm, once established, is what separates the founder haunted by panic from the one who quietly, steadily keeps more of what they earn.

Three Levers: Structure, Records, Timing

In the early years of the twentieth century, Andrew Carnegie—already one of the wealthiest men in America—was once asked what separated enduring businesses from those that collapsed in debt. His answer was deceptively plain: *"Discipline in structure, in records, in timing. Nothing more."* A century on, in a landscape infinitely more complex, his words retain their force. Success in managing taxes does not hinge on genius. It rests on three levers that any founder can pull: the legal structure chosen, the quality of the records kept, and the discipline with which obligations are timed. They are not glamorous, and they lack the allure of clever loopholes whispered about in co-working spaces. But they form the bedrock on which predictability and confidence are built.

The paradox is striking. Many founders expend enormous energy seeking arcane tax "hacks," convinced there must be secret manoeuvres hidden from view. Yet those who consistently make ordinary choices in these three domains—form, records, and calendar—outperform the brilliant but erratic. It is the rhythm of competence, not the flash of occasional brilliance, that secures stability. Just as a steady pulse keeps a body alive, so these levers keep a business financially sustainable.

Take structure. The decision whether to remain a sole trader or to incorporate is often framed in terms of prestige or credibility: the assumption that a "real company" must bear the suffix of Ltd or Inc. But in tax reality, structure governs the channels through which money flows, the way liabilities are calculated, and the options available for reinvestment or personal withdrawal. A sole trader may enjoy simplicity and lower administrative burdens but will bear unlimited personal liability. A limited company introduces formality and potentially more favourable tax rates, but with additional reporting requirements. The choice is not about vanity; it is about matching form to circumstance. Choosing wisely—and revisiting the choice as revenues grow—prevents years of costly misalignment.

Records are the second lever, and here the gap between aspiration and reality is wide. Many founders imagine record-keeping as a bureaucratic nuisance, something to be endured at year's end. Yet poor records are not merely inconvenient; they are corrosive. Without clarity on income and expenses, a founder cannot forecast cash flow, price services properly, or substantiate deductions under scrutiny. The tragedy is that records decay by default: every day that passes without logging a transaction makes it harder to recall, reconstruct, and defend. Conversely, a modest, consistent record-keeping habit compounds in value. A receipt photographed today, a note scribbled on an invoice tomorrow, a simple spreadsheet maintained weekly—these small acts accumulate into resilience. They are the difference between a frantic reconstruction and an orderly archive.

The third lever—timing—might be the most underestimated of all. Taxes are not merely about amounts; they are about *when*. Income recognised in December rather than January may alter an entire year's liability. Quarterly payments made on schedule preserve cash flow; missed by weeks, they accrue penalties and interest. Even the cadence of internal practices—weekly reconciliations, monthly reviews—changes outcomes more than most realise. Timing is a discipline of rhythm: the willingness to align financial acts with the external calendar of authorities, and to keep that alignment steady regardless of the distractions of business life. It is rarely dramatic, but it is often decisive.

To see the force of these levers, consider two contrasting freelancers. The first, brilliant in her craft, treats tax as an afterthought. She operates without a clear legal structure, shifting income and expenses through personal accounts. Receipts sit in a shoebox, reconciled only under duress. Quarterly deadlines are noticed only when reminders arrive. She is capable of dazzling work for her clients, yet her financial life is chaotic. Each year brings panic, unexpected liabilities, and the steady erosion of trust in her own competence.

The second freelancer is no more gifted, but she operates differently. She chose a structure that fits her scale and risk. She logs income and expenses weekly, using basic software and a business-only bank account. She sets calendar reminders for quarterly payments and treats them as non-negotiable. She rarely optimises in dramatic ways, yet she consistently meets obligations with confidence. Over time, her steadiness compounds into advantage: lower penalties, clearer pricing, and the psychological freedom of knowing that her system will not betray her.

The contrast illustrates the deeper point. Taxes reward consistency over brilliance. They are less like a chess game, with brilliant tactical manoeuvres, and more like a marathon, where finishing depends on steady pacing. Sporadic brilliance—an ingenious deduction spotted once, an elaborate loophole exploited briefly—cannot compensate for chronic neglect in structure, records, or timing. The founder who masters the levers builds durability; the one who ignores them courts fragility.

There is also a philosophical insight embedded here. Human beings are drawn to novelty and to drama. We admire bold moves and rare insights. Yet in fields governed by systems—whether in health, in law, or in tax—it is discipline that wins. The three levers exemplify this truth. They are not secrets but practices. They do not promise glamour but stability. In that stability lies the freedom to focus on what truly matters: building, creating, and living without the constant hum of financial dread.

Still, these levers pose a challenge, precisely because they demand the kind of attention that feels unremarkable. To choose structure wisely requires reflection rather than haste. To maintain records requires a tolerance for small, repetitive actions. To honour timing requires humility before the calendar. None of these is dramatic, but each resists our natural impulses. It is easier to fantasise about loopholes than to photograph receipts; easier to postpone than to reconcile. The question, then, is whether a founder is willing to embrace the unglamorous disciplines that pay off in durability.

Carnegie's century-old observation remains apt: enduring businesses are built on discipline, not spectacle. The founder's challenge is to resist the seduction of sporadic brilliance and to lean instead on the steady pull of three levers. The rewards are not immediate fireworks but long-term confidence: the ability to look at tax not as a source of panic, but as a managed rhythm within the life of the business.

And yet, a lingering tension remains. If these levers are so clear, why are they so often ignored? Why do intelligent people still chase the glitter of loopholes, or allow receipts to languish, or miss deadlines that were printed plainly in advance? Perhaps because the levers are too ordinary, too lacking in drama to capture attention. Perhaps because human beings are wired to undervalue prevention in favour of crisis. Or perhaps because we prefer the illusion of brilliance to the quiet labour of discipline. The questions remain, and their answers will shape not only how much founders keep of what they earn, but how securely they build the foundations on which their ventures rest.

Country-Agnostic Rules vs Local Quirks

A founder in Toronto, a freelancer in Bangalore, and a consultant in London may all open their laptops on the same morning to face the same basic question: *is this expense deductible?* Yet by the time each of them has answered it, they may have travelled entirely different paths. The Canadian might find herself navigating the intricacies of capital cost allowances. The Indian professional confronts depreciation blocks under the Income Tax Act. The Brit consults guidance on annual investment allowances. And the American must decide whether to apply Section 179 expensing or bonus depreciation. The surface question is identical; the answers are shaped by the jurisdiction.

This dissonance is what paralyses many first-time founders. They imagine tax as a labyrinth of local rules, each detail a potential trap, each exception demanding exhaustive study. The result is either overconfidence—assuming their home country's rules apply everywhere—or despair, convinced the whole subject is impenetrable. Yet there is a subtler truth: beneath the clutter of local quirks, the skeleton of taxation is remarkably consistent. Income is taxable when it is earned or received. Expenses are deductible if they are ordinary, necessary, and demonstrable. Capital investments are treated differently from consumables. These principles travel. The art lies in recognising when a general rule applies and when to pause and check for a local deviation.

This distinction is more than a matter of efficiency; it is the difference between confidence and chaos. A founder who internalises the universal rules can operate calmly across borders, knowing when their footing is secure. They do not drown in exceptions because they have a map of the terrain. The exceptions become manageable precisely because the underlying framework is stable. In this sense, understanding the portability of tax rules is both a practical and a philosophical achievement: it transforms the world from a patchwork of arbitrary demands into a system with discernible order.

Take income recognition as a case in point. Whether in the United States, the United Kingdom, Canada, or India, the central question is always *when* income is counted. The two models—cash and accrual—exist in every system, even if defaults vary. Cash basis recognises income when money is received, expenses when paid. Accrual basis recognises them when earned or incurred, regardless of when cash moves. The terms may differ, thresholds for eligibility may shift, but the logic is the same. The universal principle is that income must be consistently matched to a method. The local quirks are thresholds, elections, and reporting formats.

Or consider expenses. The United States speaks of "ordinary and necessary." The United Kingdom of "wholly and exclusively." Canada asks whether costs are "reasonable." India refers to "expenditure incurred wholly and exclusively for business." The language shifts, but the principle is constant: the expense must be genuinely tied to the business, not a disguised personal indulgence. What varies is how strictly authorities interpret categories like meals, travel, or home-office use. The founder who grasps the underlying rule can evaluate expenses with confidence, consulting local notes only when categories blur.

The distinction is equally clear in the treatment of capital expenditure. Every jurisdiction draws a line between items consumed quickly and assets that endure. A pen is an expense; a laptop is capital. The methods diverge—depreciation schedules in India, capital cost allowance classes in Canada, annual investment allowances in the UK, accelerated expensing in the US—but the conceptual frame is shared. The universal principle is that durable assets are not written off immediately; the local quirk is how fast and under what conditions they can be.

Why does this matter? Because without recognising universals, founders drown in detail. They become paralysed by memorising forms, thresholds, and terminology, without seeing the continuity beneath. By contrast, a founder who grasps the portable principles can make decisions swiftly, deferring only those few where quirks truly matter. It is the difference between driving with a clear sense of direction and creeping forward at every junction because the road signs look unfamiliar.

There is also a psychological dividend in separating the general from the local. Much of tax panic stems from the fear of missing some obscure detail. But once you see that 80 per cent of rules are stable across contexts, the fear recedes. The remaining 20 per cent—thresholds, elections, and reporting forms—becomes a finite set of exceptions rather than an infinite unknown. Confidence grows not from mastering every quirk, but from knowing when to ask, *is this a universal or a local?*

Still, the tension remains. Nations are jealous of their sovereignty, and tax codes are among the most guarded expressions of it. Each government tweaks rules to encourage or discourage behaviours, to raise revenue without losing popularity, to align with domestic politics. These quirks are not noise; they are deliberate signals of national policy. A Canadian small business deduction, a UK dividend allowance, an Indian goods and services tax threshold—each encodes political choices. To operate internationally, founders must respect these signals without letting them obscure the universals. The art is not to deny local colour, but to treat it as detail layered on a stable canvas.

The motif of "rules that travel" versus "quirks that stick" is more than a practical sorting tool. It reflects something deeper about human systems. Most of life operates on shared principles—fair exchange, reciprocity, stewardship—yet every culture dresses them in different garments. The founder who sees taxation as a microcosm of this truth acquires more than financial literacy; they acquire cultural fluency. They learn to distinguish essence from expression, substance from form.

And yet the unresolved question lingers: why do so many founders ignore universals and obsess over quirks? Perhaps because quirks feel more concrete, more tangible—thresholds and forms you can point to—while universals feel abstract. Perhaps because advice markets thrive on novelty, selling the latest twist in one jurisdiction rather than the timeless rules that underpin them all. Or perhaps because it is human nature to find comfort in detail even when it distracts from the larger frame.

Whatever the reason, the challenge stands. Will you allow yourself to drown in exceptions, always chasing the peculiarities of each code? Or will you internalise the rules that travel, using them as your compass, and consult the quirks only when the road bends? The answer will determine not only your competence across jurisdictions but your confidence in every decision that touches tax. The world may be fragmented by sovereignty, but its financial skeleton is strikingly unified. To see that clearly is to gain an advantage few ever claim.

From Fear to a Weekly Ritual

Every founder remembers the first time tax caught them off guard. It is rarely the headline figures that sting most, but the timing: the letter that lands after months of silence, the payment deadline that suddenly looms when cash is already committed elsewhere. The paradox is cruel. For weeks or months, everything seems calm, almost forgettable; then, in a single afternoon, dread collapses in like a wave. Some describe it as though a spotlight had been turned on their financial life, revealing every neglected receipt, every postponed decision, every hour of avoidance. Panic takes root not because the numbers are insurmountable, but because the founder realises, too late, that they were predictable all along.

And yet, the difference between panic and confidence can be as modest as half an hour a week. A simple ritual, done consistently, transforms tax from an unpredictable ambush into a managed routine. Capture income. Classify expenses. Move money into a tax set-aside. Glance at the calendar. Thirty minutes, no more. Small enough to fit between meetings, yet powerful enough to prevent the late-night scrambles that define the experience of so many entrepreneurs.

The idea that something as daunting as tax can be tamed by such a small ritual is almost offensive to those who have suffered under its weight. How can thirty minutes compete with the chaos of year-end accounts or the fines of missed deadlines? The answer lies not in the ritual's size but in its rhythm. By embedding tax discipline into a weekly cadence, founders remove the psychological traps that make obligations overwhelming. Instead of deferring pain to the future, they deal with small increments in the present. The mountain becomes a series of hills; the dread becomes habit.

Consider the first element: capturing income. It sounds obvious, but many businesses fail here. Payments come in through multiple platforms, currencies fluctuate, fees are deducted at source. A founder may know roughly how much they earned last month but lack precision. Logging income weekly prevents drift. It also forces recognition: not just what has been earned, but what remains outstanding. Unpaid invoices are noticed sooner, platform delays tracked more carefully. In this way, the ritual strengthens cash flow awareness as much as tax readiness.

The second step, classifying expenses, seems tedious until one sees its cumulative effect. Misclassified or forgotten expenses are effectively donations to the tax authority. They inflate profit on paper and liability in reality. By reviewing receipts weekly—photographing them, noting purpose, tagging categories—the founder prevents leakage. It also alters behaviour. Knowing expenses will be reviewed soon discourages careless spending and prompts better justification at the moment of purchase. What feels like bookkeeping becomes decision-shaping.

The third step, updating the tax set-aside, addresses perhaps the most corrosive trap of all: loss aversion. As behavioural economists remind us, paying money today for a benefit months away feels like pain without relief. But transferring a smaller amount weekly is less brutal than surrendering a lump sum quarterly. The jar on the shelf—whether literal or metaphorical—becomes a visible assurance that the liability is covered. It reframes payment not as sudden loss but as steady preparation. Over time, the psychological shift is profound: tax ceases to feel like theft from the future and becomes simply another cost of doing business, already accounted for.

Finally, the weekly glance at the calendar ties everything together. Deadlines no longer arrive as ambushes but appear weeks in advance, like distant landmarks on a familiar path. The founder knows when filings are due, when instalments must be made, and when records will be handed to an accountant. This small act of foresight prevents the classic founder's lament: "If only I'd known sooner." They *did* know sooner—because they looked.

What is striking about this ritual is its ordinariness. There is nothing sophisticated in photographing a receipt or setting aside a fraction of income. Yet ordinariness is its strength. Tax panic thrives in chaos and neglect; ritual thrives in repetition. The founder who treats tax as a weekly practice acquires the same advantage as an athlete who trains regularly or a musician who rehearses daily. Competence becomes muscle memory. By the time deadlines arrive, there is no scramble, because the work has been done all along.

There is also a deeper philosophical truth here. Rituals, in every culture, exist to tame the unknown. They turn chaos into order by anchoring meaning in repeated acts. The weekly tax ritual may lack incense and chant, but it serves the same function. It transforms a domain notorious for dread into one governed by rhythm. Fear dissipates not because the system changes, but because the founder's posture towards it does. What was once a looming threat becomes part of the weekly cadence of work, as ordinary as checking email or planning meetings.

Yet one tension remains. If the ritual is so simple, why do so few adopt it? Perhaps because the very ordinariness makes it easy to dismiss. Founders crave breakthroughs, not routines. They would rather hunt for clever deductions than spend thirty minutes each week capturing receipts. They would rather hope chaos can be managed in bursts than commit to steady discipline. The result is predictable: panic repeated annually, fines paid unnecessarily, confidence eroded steadily.

The challenge, then, is not intellectual but behavioural. Will the founder embrace the modesty of ritual, trusting in its compounding power, or will they cling to cycles of avoidance punctuated by crisis? The answer determines not only their tax outcomes but their relationship to discipline itself. For in the end, the weekly ritual is not just about finance. It is about the kind of life one chooses: reactive or prepared, panicked or steady.

And so the question is left hanging. What if the difference between tax as fear and tax as routine is only thirty minutes a week? Would you take it? Or will you allow the silence of avoidance to continue until the next deadline arrives, merciless and late? The choice is deceptively small, but its consequences are anything but.

Chapter 2
Choosing a Structure Without Regret

One of the most consequential decisions a founder makes is also one of the least glamorous: how to structure the business. Unlike a product launch, there is no fanfare, no marketing splash, no customer applause. Yet the choice of form—sole trader or company, partnership or limited liability entity—shapes everything that follows: how money flows, how risk is absorbed, how taxes are paid, and how long the founder can sleep at night without fearing a letter from the authorities. Paradoxically, the decision is often made for the wrong reasons. A friend insists that "real businesses" must incorporate. An adviser warns against premature complexity. The result is a landscape littered with founders who either incorporated too soon, locking themselves into compliance burdens they could not afford, or who clung to sole proprietorship for too long, exposing themselves to unnecessary personal risk. Regret is the silent companion of poor structuring.

Consider the case of a London consultant who incorporated within weeks of winning her first client, persuaded that the "Ltd" suffix would add credibility. The reality was a maze of filings, payroll set-ups, and tax obligations that swallowed her first year's surplus. Contrast this with the Toronto designer who, despite growing revenue, clung to sole proprietorship out of fear of paperwork, only to discover that she had overpaid in taxes for years, missing out on the small business deductions available to Canadian corporations. Both were intelligent, both hardworking, both sincere in their ambitions. Their errors lay not in ability but in mismatched structure. They illustrate a wider truth: form matters less as a label and more as a channel through which cash, risk, and compliance flow.

What complicates the matter is that structure is not static. A sole trader may be perfect for early months, where cash flow is volatile and risk minimal. But as revenue stabilises, as employees are hired, as contracts grow in size, the calculus changes. Liability protection becomes essential, tax rate progression grows significant, and the discipline of separate banking and payroll systems begins to pay dividends. Conversely, incorporation too soon can smother agility, burdening a founder with costs and filings that sap energy from the work itself. Timing is as important as form. Knowing when to switch—guided by revenue thresholds, risk exposure, or hiring decisions—turns what might have been a source of regret into a tool of resilience.

The second axis of choice is not about structure itself, but about extraction: how the founder pays themselves. Here, too, instinct misleads. Many reach for simplicity: withdraw money when needed. Others attempt cleverness: minimise salary, maximise dividends, or pursue an arrangement whispered about in online forums. Yet the truth is that the way money leaves the business is often where tax bites hardest. Salary, draws, and dividends each carry different implications for cash flow, tax liability, and paperwork. A company making the same profit can end with three very different after-tax results depending on which method is chosen. More importantly, compensation is not just about minimising liability; it is about aligning with stability, compliance, and long-term wealth. To treat extraction as mere "owner's pay" is to miss its strategic force.

And then there is the overlooked foundation: set-up itself. Too many founders treat incorporation as a matter of paperwork alone, rushing through forms without setting up the systems that prevent future pain. Registrations half-completed, tax accounts opened too late, payroll IDs missing, or personal and business funds commingled—these small oversights create long shadows. They re-emerge at audit, at financing rounds, or when a client demands due diligence. A clean foundation, by contrast, pays dividends for years: separate banking accounts that make reconciliation simple, payroll systems that unlock retirement contributions, resolutions that formalise decisions before disputes arise. The set-up checklist is not bureaucracy; it is insurance against future regret.

What emerges from all of this is a pattern. Founders who approach structure as a box-ticking exercise—something to be done quickly and forgotten—inevitably face headaches later. Those who treat it as a living decision, revisited with growth, aligned with cash flow, risk, and paperwork discipline, find themselves on firmer ground. The rewards are subtle but significant: cash preserved, liabilities managed, audits endured without panic.

The deeper lesson is that structure is less about labels than about impact. Whether you call it an LLC, a Ltd, a Canadian corporation, or an Indian LLP, the essence is the same: a framework that shapes the flow of money and responsibility. To focus on the name alone is to miss the point; to focus on the effects is to act with clarity.

The question for every founder, then, is not "What structure looks most impressive?" but "What structure serves me best—today, and tomorrow?" The answer will rarely be final, and that is its strength. Structures can change; timing can be adjusted; systems can be improved. The goal is not perfection but prevention: avoiding the traps of premature incorporation and costly inertia. And as with so much in the world of tax, the reward lies not in brilliance but in rhythm—the steady discipline of aligning form, pay, and systems with the evolving shape of the business.

But a lingering tension remains. If the choices are so pivotal, why do so many founders make them casually, or delay them entirely? Perhaps because structure feels abstract compared to the immediacy of clients and cash. Perhaps because it lacks the thrill of product launches or the urgency of sales calls. Yet the irony is that the future stability of the business depends on precisely these invisible foundations. And so the chapter begins with a challenge: will you treat structure as a burden to be postponed, or as a lever to be pulled with intention? The answer, as you will see, determines not only how much of what you earn you keep, but how securely you build the platform on which your venture rests.

Sole Trader vs Company: Decision Criteria That Matter

A curious irony defines the early life of many founders: they obsess over the colour of a logo or the font on a website, yet make the structural decision of their business with a shrug. "Just set up a company," someone advises, and the paperwork is filed. Or, conversely, they stick to a sole proprietorship because it seems simpler, not realising the long shadow this choice can cast. Years later, some discover that premature incorporation saddled them with needless compliance burdens and cash-flow strain. Others realise that clinging to sole trader status exposed them to personal liability or higher taxes than necessary. Few regret their product; many regret their structure.

The heart of the decision is not glamour but impact. Whether you trade as a sole proprietor, form a limited company, elect an S-corp in the United States, incorporate in Canada, or register an LLP in India, the label itself is secondary. What matters is how the choice affects four things: cash flow, liability, administrative burden, and tax rate progression. These are the levers that shape not only how much of what you earn you keep, but how resilient your business becomes in the face of shocks.

Take cash flow. A sole trader typically enjoys simplicity: income flows directly into personal accounts, tax is paid through self-assessment, and compliance costs are low. The downside is that profits are taxed as personal income in full, with few opportunities to defer or smooth liabilities. By contrast, a company may allow income splitting between salary and dividends, or access to lower corporate rates at certain thresholds. Yet the trade-off is liquidity restriction. Money is no longer "yours" until it passes through formal channels, often involving payroll or dividend declarations. For some, that discipline is a virtue; for others, it feels like a straitjacket.

Liability is the second pillar. The difference between personal and limited liability is not theoretical. A sole trader is personally responsible for debts, lawsuits, or fines. A client dispute or an unpaid supplier can spill over into personal savings or even a family home. Incorporation introduces a shield—imperfect, but meaningful. The company becomes the debtor, not the individual. In industries with higher risk—construction, consultancy, health services—this shield can mean survival. Yet it is no panacea. Directors can still be held personally liable for negligence or fraud. The shield protects, but it does not absolve.

Administrative burden forms the third consideration. Sole traders usually contend with a single tax return, light bookkeeping, and minimal filings. This simplicity is seductive, especially in the frenetic early days when every spare minute belongs to sales or product development. But simplicity can conceal fragility. Incorporation, by contrast, demands more: statutory accounts, annual returns, payroll systems, often professional support. At first glance, these obligations look like anchors. Yet for many businesses, they become scaffolding. They enforce separation of personal and business funds, create cleaner records, and build credibility with banks, investors, and clients. What feels like bureaucracy can, in practice, be the discipline that sustains growth.

Finally, there is the matter of tax rate progression. A sole trader's profits are taxed on a sliding personal scale. At lower levels, this may be efficient. At higher levels, it can become punitive. Companies often benefit from flat or lower corporate rates, with additional flexibility in how profits are distributed. In the United States, the S-corp election allows income to flow directly to owners, avoiding double taxation. In the United Kingdom, the combination of salary and dividends can optimise both tax and national insurance contributions. In Canada, the small business deduction reduces rates for eligible corporations. In India, LLPs offer partnership flexibility with limited liability, while private limited companies open doors to equity investment but impose heavier compliance. The details differ, but the principle is constant: structure shapes progression, and progression shapes outcomes.

The mistake many founders make is to see these criteria in isolation. They choose incorporation solely for the promise of lower tax rates, ignoring the cash-flow rigidity or administrative burden. Or they remain sole traders to preserve simplicity, overlooking exposure to liability or the long-term tax costs of rising profits. The wiser approach is to see the interplay. Sometimes the stability of corporate discipline outweighs the immediate simplicity of sole trading. At other times, the freedom of sole trader status outweighs the marginal savings of incorporation. Context is everything: revenue level, industry risk, growth trajectory, personal appetite for complexity.

What unites these considerations is the need to prioritise impact over labels. Calling a business an LLC or a Ltd may sound impressive, but the title itself is meaningless unless it aligns with cash, liability, paperwork, and rates. Structure should serve the business, not the ego. Too often, founders incorporate for the optics, believing that clients will take them more seriously. Sometimes they do. But credibility earned by delivery is stronger than credibility borrowed from suffixes. Conversely, some delay incorporation out of inertia, convinced that complexity will kill their momentum, only to find that the cost of waiting was higher than the cost of switching earlier.

The philosophical challenge here is one of humility. Structure will not make a bad business succeed, nor will it ruin a good one overnight. But it will tilt the playing field, subtly and persistently. A business with the wrong form bleeds unnecessarily—through tax, through risk, through inefficiency. A business with the right form gains durability: cash retained, liabilities contained, compliance harnessed as discipline. The founder's task is not to guess the "perfect" structure but to choose the one that serves best at the current stage, with an eye to when the calculus will shift.

And this leads to the most difficult tension of all: when to change. Incorporating too soon can suffocate cash flow; waiting too long can create exposure or lost savings. There is no universal threshold, only patterns: rising profits that tip into higher brackets, contracts that demand limited liability, teams that require payroll systems. Each signal whispers that the balance has shifted, that what once served must now evolve. The founder who listens to these signals avoids regret; the one who ignores them eventually pays a price.

So the question hangs: what will guide your choice—labels or impact, ego or effect? The forms are many, the labels endless, but the criteria are stable: cash, liability, burden, progression. They are not glamorous, but they are decisive. Every founder must answer them, explicitly or by default. And the cost of answering wrongly is not theoretical; it is lived in sleepless nights, wasted money, and unnecessary risk. The real test, then, is not whether you can name your structure but whether you can explain why it truly serves you now—and when you will know it is time to change.

Pay Yourself: Salary, Draw, or Dividend

There is a peculiar irony at the heart of entrepreneurship: the business exists to generate income, yet the founder often struggles to decide how to take it home. They may be adept at pricing, skilled at negotiation, or visionary in product design, but when it comes to extracting their own reward, hesitation creeps in. Should the money be treated as salary, withdrawn as a draw, or distributed as a dividend? Each path alters the arithmetic, the paperwork, and even the founder's perception of stability. Few questions feel so intimate yet carry such wide-ranging consequences.

Consider a founder in Chicago who built her company to six figures in profit. She opted for dividends, convinced they would minimise her tax. On paper, she was correct—her liability fell. In practice, she found herself unable to secure a mortgage because lenders treated dividend income as unstable. Across the ocean in Manchester, another founder insisted on paying himself only through salary, valuing the predictability of a payslip. Yet he paid more tax than necessary, draining cash from the business that might have fuelled growth. In Bangalore, a sole proprietor blurred the lines entirely, drawing cash ad hoc whenever expenses arose, until the absence of discipline left him scrambling at year-end. These stories are not outliers; they illustrate a universal truth. The method of extraction is not a technicality—it shapes the founder's financial life, their compliance posture, and the culture of their business.

At its core, the choice reflects a tension between flexibility and formality. Salary offers stability: a predictable flow, deductions handled at source, pension eligibility intact. It sends a signal of seriousness to banks, partners, and employees. Yet it locks in costs, creates payroll obligations, and exposes income to higher rates of personal tax in many jurisdictions. Draws, by contrast, offer fluidity. A sole trader can pull cash as needed without the trappings of payroll, but this informality breeds risk. Without discipline, draws can obscure true profitability, leading to unpleasant surprises when tax authorities demand their share. Dividends sit between the two—formal enough to require declarations, yet flexible in timing, often taxed more lightly than salaries. But dividends carry restrictions: they can only be paid from profits, not cash alone, and their perception in credit assessments or government benefits can be limiting.

The complexity deepens across jurisdictions. In the United States, S-corporation owners often split extraction: a "reasonable" salary subject to payroll tax, supplemented by distributions that avoid it. In the United Kingdom, the salary–dividend mix is a familiar dance, with many directors paying themselves a minimal salary to secure national insurance credits and topping up with dividends to benefit from lower tax rates. In Canada, the choice is equally strategic: dividends can be tax-efficient but forgo retirement contributions; salaries generate RRSP room but increase payroll burden. In India, where proprietors and LLP partners often rely on draws, incorporation into a private limited company shifts the balance, enabling salaries or dividends but imposing corporate formalities. The mechanics vary, but the tension remains: stability against efficiency, formality against flexibility.

What complicates matters further is that the optimal choice is rarely permanent. In the early days, when cash is volatile and profits uncertain, draws may feel natural. Later, as profits grow and external scrutiny increases, a salary builds credibility. Still later, dividends may provide a means to fine-tune extraction without straining liquidity. Founders who cling rigidly to one method risk misalignment with their own stage of growth. What serves at £30,000 profit may hinder at £300,000. The method must evolve with the business.

And yet, many founders fall into the trap of chasing the theoretical minimum. They calculate which method shaves the most off their tax bill this year and pursue it doggedly, regardless of wider consequences. But this fixation can backfire. The founder who minimises salary to save tax may later struggle with pension shortfalls or loan approvals. The one who avoids dividends entirely may forgo flexibility that could smooth cash flow. The one who treats draws as casual transfers may attract scrutiny for blurred lines between business and personal finances. The pursuit of the lowest liability often undermines stability, credibility, and compliance—the very pillars on which long-term wealth depends.

What emerges is a more nuanced philosophy. Paying oneself is not just a financial calculation; it is a behavioural signal. It shapes how the founder perceives their role, how others perceive the business, and how resilient the enterprise becomes under scrutiny. A payslip suggests permanence. A dividend suggests reward. A draw suggests immediacy. Each carries symbolic weight beyond the numbers. Extraction is thus both arithmetic and narrative: a story told through money about what the business is, and what it intends to be.

Perhaps the real question, then, is not *which method saves the most tax* but *which method aligns with the founder's broader objectives*. Is the goal to build credibility with lenders? To preserve maximum flexibility for reinvestment? To balance immediate cash needs with future retirement security? Each answer points towards a different mix. And in practice, many founders discover that balance, not purity, is the solution: a modest salary to anchor stability, dividends to fine-tune efficiency, and—where appropriate—draws for informal adjustments. The art lies in crafting the mix deliberately, rather than stumbling into it by default.

Yet the unresolved tension remains. How much weight should one give to today's tax saving versus tomorrow's financial resilience? Is it better to be lean now and risk difficulty later, or to shoulder higher costs today for the sake of credibility and security? The tax code offers options, but it does not answer this question. That responsibility lies with the founder. And it is here, in the quiet decision of how to pay oneself, that the wider drama of entrepreneurship plays out: discipline versus freedom, immediacy versus foresight, personal need versus institutional form.

The money is already earned. The question is how it should arrive in your pocket—and what story that choice will tell about you and your business.

When It's Time to Switch Forms

Every founder eventually encounters a moment that feels oddly anticlimactic. Revenue climbs, clients multiply, or investors take interest, and suddenly the structure that once seemed perfectly adequate feels fragile. A sole trader whose biggest expense used to be a laptop now signs contracts worth six figures. A partnership once based on trust between friends begins to creak under the strain of new staff and complex liabilities. What began as freedom begins to feel like exposure. The paradox is striking: the very success that validates the business also destabilises the form in which it is held.

History offers countless examples of institutions that collapsed not for lack of vision, but for clinging too long to forms that no longer served them. Media companies built for print struggled in the digital age, guilds and associations crumbled when trade globalised, and family-run enterprises faltered when inheritance collided with scale. The lesson is universal: structures that work at one stage can become liabilities at another. The founder who recognises this truth and adapts in time avoids crises that destroy slower-moving peers.

For the modern entrepreneur, this recognition begins with thresholds. Revenue, profit, and risk are not just numbers on a report; they are signals that the current form is nearing its limits. A UK freelancer who once billed £30,000 annually as a sole trader might manage comfortably under self-assessment. But when profits approach six figures, the combination of rising income tax, national insurance, and the availability of dividend allowances begins to shift the equation. A Canadian designer who exceeds the small business deduction threshold may suddenly find incorporation far more efficient, not just in tax terms but in signalling stability to clients and banks. An Indian consultant whose LLP remains lean may outgrow it when private limited company status becomes essential for raising outside capital. The details differ, but the principle is consistent: growth changes the stakes, and the structure must evolve with it.

Risk, too, sharpens the case for change. In the early days, when a founder consults with a handful of clients and carries little inventory, personal liability may seem manageable. But when contracts involve deliverables with legal exposure, when employees are hired, or when operations expand internationally, the personal shield offered by incorporation shifts from theoretical to essential. The distinction between "I am the business" and "the business is its own entity" becomes not just semantic but existential. A lawsuit, a debt default, or a regulatory penalty that once might have been survivable can become ruinous without the buffer of limited liability.

There is also the matter of credibility. However much one may disdain appearances, the reality is that form signals seriousness. A company suffix—Ltd, Inc., Pvt Ltd—can reassure corporate clients, investors, or lenders that they are dealing with an organisation rather than a hobbyist. Banks prefer payroll slips to ad hoc drawings; investors prefer shares to vague promises of ownership. Incorporation is not, in itself, a mark of substance, but it is a language understood by the wider economic world. Founders who refuse to "dress" their structure appropriately risk being misunderstood, even if their underlying business is sound.

Yet there is danger on the other side of the spectrum: moving too soon. Incorporation brings with it administrative burdens—statutory filings, payroll accounts, directors' resolutions—that can drain time and money. The founder who rushes to incorporate for prestige alone may find themselves spending more on compliance than they save in tax. Worse, premature complexity can distract from the work of actually building the business. A lean sole trader with modest income may be better served by simplicity than by the trappings of corporate formality. Here lies the tension: switch too late, and you bleed through liability or excess tax; switch too early, and you suffocate in bureaucracy.

The most resilient founders navigate this tension not by waiting for perfection but by recognising trigger points. Revenue consistently surpassing personal tax thresholds. Hiring employees whose wages must be managed through formal systems. Signing contracts whose risk profiles demand limited liability. Seeking capital from investors who require equity structures. Each of these is a signal that the old form is nearing obsolescence. None offers a precise calendar date, but together they form a compass. The founder who listens avoids both costly inertia and premature complexity.

Philosophically, the act of switching forms is an act of maturity. It acknowledges that the business is no longer simply an extension of the founder's will, but an entity in its own right. This shift can be uncomfortable. Many founders resist incorporation not because of paperwork but because of the subtle identity change it entails: from individual to institution. To embrace that change is to accept the discipline and responsibility of building something larger than oneself. To resist it indefinitely is to cling to a freedom that may, paradoxically, limit growth.

And yet the question lingers: how does one know with certainty that the moment has come? There is no definitive test, no single threshold that applies to all. What exists instead are patterns, signals, and the founder's own readiness to trade simplicity for resilience.

The decision is less about chasing tax efficiency than about aligning structure with stage. The wrong form does not always destroy a business overnight, but it erodes its stability, undermines its capacity to endure shocks, and leaves its owner perpetually vulnerable.

So the founder must decide: will you wait until circumstance forces your hand—through a tax bill too high, a liability too great, a deal lost to a competitor with a more formal structure—or will you act before necessity turns into regret? The moment of switching form rarely feels urgent until it is too late. The real discipline lies in seeing the inevitability of change before it arrives, and preparing for it with intention. The form you choose is not forever, but the cost of choosing late can echo for years.

Set-up checklist that prevents future pain

One of the cruellest tricks in business is how invisible foundations remain until the day they collapse. For years, a founder can glide along without a separate bank account, without proper payroll registrations, without anything more formal than receipts shoved into a drawer. It feels nimble, resourceful, even romantic. Then, at the worst possible moment—an audit, a funding round, a dispute with a partner—the house built on sand gives way. Suddenly, the costs of shortcuts compound into sleepless nights and existential threats. What looked like freedom was fragility all along.

History is littered with cautionary tales of enterprises undone not by poor sales or bad ideas, but by administrative neglect. In the nineteenth century, small trading houses collapsed not because ships failed to arrive but because ledgers were chaotic, creditors uncertain, and obligations unenforceable. Today, the equivalents are unpaid payroll liabilities, confused tax accounts, or partners without clear resolutions. The mechanics differ, but the principle is identical: without a solid foundation, the edifice of enterprise buckles under the smallest shock.

The temptation to cut corners at the outset is understandable. After all, no founder starts a business out of passion for forms, registrations, and banking rituals. Yet these modest, often tedious tasks are not dead paperwork—they are the architecture of resilience. They separate the fragile experiment from the enterprise that can endure storms. By taking them seriously, a founder doesn't just comply with regulations; they lay down habits that prevent future pain, reduce decision fatigue, and create trust with every stakeholder from tax authorities to investors.

Consider the act of registering properly with tax authorities. It may feel perfunctory, even redundant, but in truth it signals the business's very existence in the legal order. A registration number is not just a code; it is an identity, the anchor that connects the business to the wider fiscal and legal ecosystem. Without it, everything downstream—filings, reliefs, even the right to defend against unfair assessments—becomes compromised. Founders who neglect this step often discover, years later, that the cost of retroactive compliance far exceeds the small inconvenience of doing it right at the start.

Separate banking is another deceptively simple step with profound consequences. Blurring personal and business accounts may save minutes in the short run, but it invites confusion and suspicion. When every coffee receipt and client payment mingles in the same stream, clarity dissolves. Tax audits become nightmares, investors recoil at the lack of separation, and the founder themselves loses the ability to truly see the business's performance. By contrast, a dedicated business account creates a clean line between personal and professional, not only making compliance easier but also reinforcing a psychological shift: this is no longer "me freelancing"; it is a business with its own life.

Payroll identifiers and systems, too, matter far earlier than many assume. Hiring one employee informally may feel harmless until questions of tax withholding, benefits, or termination arise. Governments do not forgive ignorance in these matters. The founder who registers properly for payroll from the outset gains more than compliance—they gain a repeatable system. Each payslip generated, each remittance made, reinforces discipline and signals professionalism to employees. It says: this organisation is real, accountable, and built to last.

Then there are the small but essential resolutions: the formal minutes and agreements that record key decisions. At first they may feel performative—why bother drafting a resolution when you and your co-founder already agreed over coffee? Yet when disputes arise, or when investors scrutinise governance, those scraps of formality become lifelines. They transform memory and goodwill into documented authority. In moments of strain, when recollections differ, the existence of a signed resolution can prevent months of bitterness and thousands in legal fees.

What ties all these elements together—registrations, tax accounts, banking separation, payroll systems, resolutions—is not bureaucracy for its own sake, but the cultivation of habits. Each step forces a founder to behave as though the business is already significant, already accountable, already worth protecting. These habits compound. The weekly reconciliation of a separate account makes quarterly filings effortless. The routine of documenting decisions builds a culture of clarity. What begins as compliance hardens into resilience.

The irony is that founders often view these steps as distractions from "real" work, when in fact they enable the very possibility of doing real work at scale. A business without clear tax registrations cannot confidently bid for contracts. A venture without payroll systems cannot reliably employ talent. A partnership without documented resolutions cannot raise external finance. Each shortcut taken at the beginning becomes a barrier at the moment growth demands legitimacy.

Philosophically, the checklist is a test of seriousness. To set up properly is to accept that the enterprise is not a temporary hustle but an enduring endeavour. It requires a shift in identity: from improvisation to institution. This shift does not strip away flexibility; it preserves it, by ensuring the business can respond to opportunities without being paralysed by regulatory panic or structural chaos. Freedom in business comes not from ignoring constraints, but from anticipating them and building systems that make them almost invisible.

And so the founder is left with a choice. Will you invest a handful of hours now—completing registrations, opening accounts, establishing payroll IDs, drafting resolutions—or will you gamble on improvisation, hoping the cracks remain hidden until success makes them impossible to ignore? The set-up checklist is not glamorous, but it is the silent scaffolding on which all later growth depends. The question is not whether you can get away without it for a while; it is how much it will cost you when you finally can't.

Chapter 3
What Counts as Income (and When)

The story is almost always the same. A founder celebrates a record-breaking quarter, contracts signed, invoices sent, the future looking brighter than ever. Then the accountant calls: the tax bill is larger than the cash sitting in the bank. How can this be? No lavish spending spree, no hidden theft—simply the brutal mismatch between when income is *recognised* and when it is actually received. That moment of shock, when profit appears on paper but liquidity vanishes in practice, has broken more promising businesses than bad products ever have.

This is not a new problem. Merchants in Renaissance Florence argued over whether revenue should be booked when cloth was sold, when it was delivered, or when the gold florins arrived in hand. The tension between "earning" and "being paid" has haunted commerce for centuries. Today, the paradox is sharper still. Digital platforms settle in uneven cycles, foreign payments can take weeks to clear, and subscription revenues trickle in monthly while expenses hit daily. What looks like growth on a chart may conceal cash starvation in reality.

At its core, the question of "what counts as income" is both technical and philosophical. It is about definitions and timing, yes, but also about fairness and survival. Tax authorities, investors, and founders themselves must all agree on when value has truly been created. A mismatch here does not just cause confusion; it determines whether a business thrives, treads water, or drowns. For the solo founder or small company, understanding these rules is not optional—it is the difference between control and chaos.

Cash versus accrual accounting provides the first, and perhaps starkest, fork in the road. In plain terms, cash accounting treats income as real only when the money is in your hands; accrual accounting, by contrast, deems income "earned" the moment an obligation is fulfilled, regardless of when payment arrives. Both methods are defensible, both are used around the world, and both can radically reshape how a balance sheet looks. The challenge is not merely in knowing the definitions, but in grasping how they map onto your obligations. A tax bill assessed on accrued income, when clients still owe you tens of thousands, is not a theoretical problem—it is a crisis of survival.

Layered on top of these timing differences are the growing complexities of modern revenue streams. A century ago, income meant sales of goods or provision of services. Today, income may mean monthly subscriptions billed automatically, platform payouts net of fees and foreign withholding, digital product royalties arriving in unpredictable bursts, or hybrid contracts blending service with licence. Each of these raises a deceptively simple question: *what is the true amount earned?* The $10,000 deposit from a platform may in fact represent $12,000 of gross revenue, less fees you never saw but are expected to account for. Misreading such flows distorts profit, margins, and ultimately the tax base itself.

Foreign income adds another dimension. For founders working across borders, exchange rates, treaty provisions, and questions of "permanent establishment" complicate the otherwise simple task of recording receipts. The euro payment that lands in your Canadian dollar account is not just income but a currency event, subject to fluctuations and reporting nuances. The client in India paying into your UK account might, in the eyes of regulators, trigger obligations you had no idea existed. Clean records are not only good practice—they are the only defence against double taxation or penalties for misreporting.

Even within domestic boundaries, edge cases abound. What of the invoice that will never be paid? The refund offered months after revenue was booked? The client credit that offsets future services? Each carries implications for how income is recognised. Count it too early, and you inflate profits, creating false comfort and overstated tax liabilities. Count it too late, and you risk under-reporting, inviting audits and penalties. Navigating these grey areas is not simply a matter of compliance; it is the craft of presenting a truthful picture of business reality.

The deeper lesson, however, is not that tax codes are complicated—though they are—but that clarity begins with discipline. A founder who establishes weekly rituals of recording, reconciling, and classifying income will not be immune to complexity, but will be armed against it. The entrepreneur who treats income recognition as a deliberate choice, rather than an afterthought, prevents the most common and most devastating form of financial pain: the surprise.

What, then, truly counts as income? Is it the moment of effort, the moment of invoice, or the moment of cash? The answer depends, as it always has, on where you stand: in law, in practice, in geography. But one truth cuts across contexts: ignorance is ruinously expensive, while awareness is liberating. To know what counts, and when, is to reclaim control over the lifeblood of the business.

And yet, as the chapter will show, each apparent rule carries exceptions, caveats, and quirks. The categories blur, the definitions shift, the obligations tighten. The founder must not only learn the distinctions but also cultivate the instincts to spot when a platform deposit is misleading, when a foreign receipt carries hidden obligations, or when an unpaid invoice deserves to be written off. The aim is not mastery of every tax code but the development of judgment: to know when you can rely on general principles and when you must seek specific advice.

The irony is that income—supposedly the most straightforward measure of business health—is in practice one of the most contested. To grasp what counts, and when, is to pierce through the fog of appearances and confront the financial reality of entrepreneurship. That reality is sometimes uncomfortable, sometimes reassuring, but always clarifying. The next pages will not remove all ambiguity, but they will arm you with the tools to prevent mismatches, to resist illusions, and to build a business resilient not only in theory but in practice. The question remains: when your next deposit hits the account, will you know what it truly means?

Recognition: cash vs accrual in plain language

Imagine a freelance designer in Toronto who has just completed a £5,000 website for a UK client. The invoice is sent in December, payment arrives in February, and tax season hovers ominously in

April. The designer celebrates the contract in December, worries in January, and relaxes when the funds finally appear in February. But the tax authority sees the story differently. Depending on the accounting method, that £5,000 may belong to December, February, or even a blended period. The tax bill may arrive long before the money does. What feels like a technicality can mean the difference between solvency and stress.

This paradox is as old as trade itself. Merchants in medieval Genoa fought over whether to treat goods shipped across the sea as sold at the port of departure or only once they reached safe harbour. Farmers have long asked whether income is realised at the time of harvest or only when crops are sold in the market. In both ancient and modern settings, the same tension emerges: does income happen when value is created, or only when cash changes hands?

The modern answer is that there are two dominant approaches, each with strengths and pitfalls: *cash accounting* and *accrual accounting*. Though they sound abstract, they describe profoundly different views of reality. Cash accounting is intuitive: income is recognised when the money hits your account, and expenses when they leave. For sole traders, freelancers, and very small businesses, this simplicity often mirrors lived experience. Accrual accounting, however, insists that income is tied to the moment it is *earned*, not when paid. An invoice sent in December is December's income, even if the client delays payment until spring. For governments and investors, this method better reflects economic activity, even if it punishes the entrepreneur's cash flow.

Consider the same consultancy earning $120,000 annually. On a cash basis, a slow-paying client can distort the books so that one quarter looks barren and another abundant. On an accrual basis, the books appear steady, but the bank balance may run dry while waiting for cheques to clear. Both views are true, and yet both are incomplete. This is why tax authorities, lenders, and investors often privilege accrual—while founders quietly cling to cash.

Jurisdictions lean in different directions. In the United States, sole proprietors default to cash accounting, while larger businesses are often compelled to use accrual once revenues cross certain thresholds. The United Kingdom allows small businesses to elect a "cash basis" up to a limit, beyond which accrual becomes mandatory. Canada similarly grants flexibility for unincorporated businesses but expects corporations to adhere to accrual principles. India, by contrast, tends to require accrual for most registered entities, though certain presumptive schemes simplify the task for micro-enterprises. These differences matter: they shape not just how books are kept, but when tax is due, and therefore how liquidity is managed.

The practical stakes are immense. A small digital agency may show a paper profit in December under accrual, triggering tax on income not yet received. If clients delay payment until March, the agency may find itself borrowing to pay taxes on money it has not collected. The inverse is also dangerous: under cash accounting, a flood of late payments in January might defer tax obligations, but it can also create the illusion of a bumper year, tempting overspending. In both cases, the founder risks being misled by timing rather than reality.

The intellectual tension here mirrors a broader human problem: do we define reality by what is promised or by what is delivered? Accrual embodies optimism and obligation—it records the world as it should be. Cash embodies scepticism and prudence—it records only what has materialised. Both are philosophies as much as methods, and the wise entrepreneur understands them as lenses rather than as rigid truths.

In practice, survival requires reconciling both views. A founder might use accrual for official reporting, satisfying tax rules and creating a realistic picture of earnings, while maintaining a parallel cash projection to manage liquidity. This dual awareness is not a luxury; it is a defence against mismatched obligations. Taxes assessed on accrual income, when cash lags, can destroy businesses that are profitable on paper but broke in practice.

The subtlety lies in timing. Income recognition is not a trivial footnote but the fulcrum on which cash flow balances. It governs when tax is due, how performance is perceived, and whether decisions are grounded in substance or illusion. To dismiss it as a technical matter is to mistake the map for the territory.

So when does revenue *really* happen? When the invoice is sent, when the payment clears, or when the promise is fulfilled? Each answer has its defenders, and each is enshrined in law somewhere. The founder's challenge is not to choose sides blindly but to recognise the stakes, understand the defaults in their jurisdiction, and align their practices with both compliance and cash flow.

The deeper question remains open: is it better to measure what the world owes you, or what the world has actually given? That unresolved tension—between accrual's faith in promises and cash's demand for proof—will continue to haunt entrepreneurs as long as there are goods to sell, services to render, and taxes to pay. The choice is not merely accounting; it is a philosophy of survival.

Mixed income: products, services, platforms

A musician in Mumbai uploads her album to a global streaming service. She wakes up weeks later to find a deposit in her bank account: not the $1,000 her sales dashboard showed, but $742. Somewhere along the chain, a platform took its cut, a payment processor shaved its fee, and a foreign government withheld tax at source. She scrolls the reports, bewildered. The money has arrived, but it is less than promised, with no clarity on what figure should appear in her tax return.

This gap between *what is earned* and *what is received* has become one of the great traps of the digital economy. For a craftsman selling furniture in a local market, revenue is obvious: a chair sold for £200 is income of £200. But for the online seller listing the same chair on Etsy or Amazon, the story is layered. The customer pays £200, the platform deducts a commission and remits perhaps £170, and if the buyer is overseas, there may be VAT, GST, or withholding tangled into the transaction. Does the artisan's income equal £200, £170, or something in between? The answer depends not only on accounting method but on the jurisdiction in which she reports.

This is no niche curiosity. Increasingly, even small businesses operate across a patchwork of products, services, and platforms. A single entrepreneur might teach online courses, sell digital templates, consult on strategy, and license photographs—each stream with its own quirks of recognition. Subscriptions blur periods: is annual income from a subscriber recognised at the point of payment, or rationed monthly across the year? Retainers paid up front may cover work not yet done. Platform payouts may combine dozens of micro-sales into one opaque lump sum. Each of these introduces friction, not only in accounting but in the very perception of whether the business is thriving.

The heart of the confusion lies in reconciliation. Founders tend to trust the bank account as reality, yet deposits often arrive net of fees and taxes withheld. Stripe, PayPal, Upwork, Spotify, Kindle Direct Publishing—each delivers funds differently. One provides gross figures and itemised deductions, another gives only net deposits with a labyrinthine export file available on request. Without discipline, the entrepreneur risks under-reporting income by mistaking *net received* as *gross earned*, or conversely, double counting by treating withheld amounts as expenses rather than pre-paid taxes. Both errors distort profit, tax, and strategy.

Case studies abound. A Canadian developer selling an app through Apple's App Store may find that Apple has already withheld a slice of tax for sales in Japan, while remitting only the balance to his account. If he books only what he receives, he under-declares income and risks audit penalties. A British copywriter paid through Upwork may see $2,000 earned, but only $1,840 arrives after the platform fee. Is the expense the $160 fee, or is her revenue $1,840? The correct treatment is to record $2,000 as income and $160 as expense, but this requires a deliberate step, not an automatic habit.

The philosophical thread here is one of *visibility versus reality*. What appears in the bank balance is only the end of a longer story of flows, deductions, and withholdings. To accept the deposit as truth is like judging a novel by its final page alone. The numbers that matter for tax and for decision-making are often hidden in the small print of platform dashboards—small print that many founders ignore until a government letter forces attention.

There is also the question of *timing*. Subscription models, now ubiquitous, compound the problem. A US software company charging $1,200 annually for access must decide: is that $1,200 this year's income, or should it be spread $100 per month across twelve months? Tax authorities in different countries lean different ways, and investors may insist on accrual recognition for a truer picture of liabilities. Meanwhile, the founder's cash reality is simply that $1,200 sits in the bank today. To reconcile these perspectives requires not only technical clarity but a mental shift: separating cash health from income recognition.

What emerges is less about technical trickery than about cultivating *discipline in classification.* Record gross income as it arises, even if platforms shave their share before you see it. Record fees explicitly, not as invisible ghosts in net deposits. Match foreign withholdings to potential credits, rather than treating them as vanished. Reconcile subscription and retainer income in line with both jurisdiction rules and commercial fairness. These are habits that protect margins and ensure that numbers reflect reality rather than illusion.

Yet the tension endures. Platforms are global by design, while tax systems remain stubbornly national. A small seller in Delhi can reach buyers in Berlin, Sydney, or San Francisco with a single click, but each sale may trigger a different interpretation of what counts as income and when. The entrepreneur, caught between digital scale and territorial rules, must navigate with care.

The deeper lesson is that mixed income streams demand more than clever accounting—they demand a mindset of curiosity and rigour. One must ask: what did the customer actually pay? What was withheld? What portion represents a platform's fee, and what is a tax already collected on your behalf? Behind these questions lies the survival of the business itself. Margins are thinner than they appear, and confidence evaporates when numbers cannot be trusted.

So the founder is left with a provocative challenge: in a world where income rarely arrives clean and whole, how do you design systems that reveal the truth, not just the residue? The answer is not simply technical; it is philosophical. It requires seeing each payment not as the end of the story but as evidence in a longer chain of obligations. And until that mindset takes root, every net deposit risks being a half-truth, inviting missteps that could cost far more than the platform's fee.

Foreign income and currency realities

A freelance software developer in Bangalore receives a payment from a client in New York. The invoice was for $10,000, but by the time the funds reach her Indian bank account, the number looks very different. Exchange rate fluctuations have eaten into the value, her payment processor has applied a hidden spread, and a slice has been withheld under US tax law. What she thought of as a straightforward contract suddenly fractures into three questions: how much did she actually earn, when is it recognised for Indian tax purposes, and what can she reclaim through treaty relief? The client is satisfied, but the freelancer faces complexity she never imagined when she clicked "accept project."

This scenario is no outlier. In an economy increasingly defined by cross-border flows, income is rarely domestic, clean, or linear. A yoga instructor in London may sell video classes to subscribers in Singapore. A Canadian designer might receive royalties from a European publishing house. A Kenyan consultant can serve clients in Dubai while hosting her website on American servers. The internet has erased borders for commerce, but tax systems remain stubbornly territorial, demanding to know where income originates, where value is created, and whether a foreign presence has become so permanent that a new layer of taxation applies.

The concept of *permanent establishment* captures this clash. Born in an age of factories and branches, it asks: at what point does a business cross the line from exporting services to operating in another country? A desk in Berlin rented by a Canadian consultancy, a dependent agent in Tokyo signing contracts on its behalf, or even a server in Dublin hosting critical operations—each may shift a firm from foreign supplier to local taxpayer. The threshold is often unclear, but the consequences are concrete: once deemed to have a permanent establishment, the business may owe corporate taxes abroad, even if its head office is thousands of miles away.

Yet before grappling with treaty clauses or permanent establishment thresholds, the entrepreneur must first get the basics right: *clean records*. Without accurate documentation of invoices, payment receipts, exchange rates applied, and taxes withheld, it is impossible to reconcile reality with reporting. Too many founders discover too late that their books reflect only what entered the bank account, ignoring withheld taxes that might be creditable or exchange differences that could be treated as gains or losses. What looks like a neat deposit is in fact an incomplete story.

Consider the treatment of foreign exchange. A UK consultant invoices €5,000 in May, when the pound is weak, but is paid in July, when sterling strengthens. The deposit in GBP looks disappointing compared to the invoice. Was the loss her fault, or simply the market's? From an accounting standpoint, the fluctuation may generate a foreign exchange loss deductible for tax, but only if tracked precisely. Conversely, gains may inflate taxable income. Without disciplined records, these differences vanish into the ether, leaving the founder exposed to hidden liabilities or missed relief.

The issue deepens with withholding taxes. Many countries compel foreign clients to withhold a slice of payment before remittance—10% in one jurisdiction, 15% in another. For the recipient, this is not a vanished cost but a pre-paid tax that can often be credited against domestic liability, provided it is properly documented. A Canadian creator receiving royalties from Germany, or an Indian engineer working for a US firm, may reclaim some or all of what was withheld. But treaty relief is no magic wand: it requires certificates of deduction, forms filed on time, and sometimes applications in both countries. Those who fail to organise proof often end up paying tax twice—once abroad and once at home.

The philosophical tension is stark: the borderless promise of digital commerce collides with the stubborn sovereignty of states. Entrepreneurs think in terms of clients and projects; tax systems think in terms of jurisdictions and source rules. A video call feels placeless, yet for the tax authority it has a location, and that location may create obligations. The very invisibility of the border to the entrepreneur is what makes the risk so dangerous.

Practical survival lies in building habits of precision. Record gross foreign receipts, not merely what arrives in the bank. Track exchange rates applied by platforms or banks. Preserve certificates of withholding, however obscure the paperwork may seem. Note where clients are based and whether their payments trigger obligations in their jurisdiction. These records become the raw material that professionals can use to determine whether treaty relief is available, whether a permanent establishment has been created, or whether local registration is required.

Yet even with discipline, uncertainty remains. A remote developer may wonder whether repeated projects for a French client constitute a French presence. An e-commerce seller may question whether a warehouse abroad tips them into taxable territory. A consultant may worry that a foreign visa trip inadvertently establishes a local base. These grey areas defy simple checklists, and the point at which ordinary compliance becomes international tax planning is often reached sooner than founders expect.

What begins as a single contract abroad can quietly expand into a portfolio of clients scattered across jurisdictions, each with its own laws, treaties, and thresholds. At that moment, clean records are no longer a matter of neat bookkeeping—they are the entrepreneur's only defence against double taxation, misinterpretation, and costly surprises.

The deeper question lingers: how can a world that trades without borders reconcile itself to tax systems built entirely upon them? Until that tension is resolved, every entrepreneur earning abroad must learn to treat foreign income not as exotic but as ordinary—worthy of the same precision, scepticism, and discipline as any domestic transaction. The bank deposit may look simple, but it carries with it a map of obligations, some visible, some hidden. The challenge is to read the map before the taxman does.

Bad debts, refunds, and credits

There is a peculiar cruelty in commerce: the work is delivered, the invoice issued, and yet the money never arrives. For the entrepreneur, this moment is more than a broken promise—it is an accounting dilemma. Should that unpaid invoice still be treated as income? Should the books reflect hope, or reality? Every business owner eventually faces this silent erosion of revenue, and how they record it can mean the difference between overstating profit and triggering tax liabilities on money that never materialised.

History offers its own warnings. During the Great Depression, thousands of small traders collapsed not because they lacked customers, but because too many customers defaulted. The paradox was stark: books full of receivables, pockets empty of cash. Even today, in an era of digital platforms and instant transfers, the same trap persists. The unpaid invoice lingers like a ghost, distorting financial statements and tempting tax authorities to assess income that was never truly earned. The real risk is not just financial—it is reputational, as careless treatment of debts and credits invites scrutiny, audits, and accusations of misreporting.

The distinction matters. A *bad debt* is an income that was once valid but has become irrecoverable. Its recognition requires proof: correspondence showing attempts at collection, a client's insolvency notice, or aged receivables records demonstrating futility. Jurisdictions vary—some demand formal write-off resolutions approved by directors, others accept the lapse of time as evidence. Without such documentation, an auditor may challenge the deduction, reassert the income, and accuse the business of massaging figures to soften reality. In tax, pessimism must be justified, not assumed.

Refunds belong to a different category. They are not debts that died but revenues reversed—an admission that the sale itself has been unwound. A retailer refunding a defective product, a consultant reimbursing an advance after a cancelled project, or a subscription platform issuing pro-rated credits to departing users: each reduces income, not by virtue of non-payment, but by undoing the original transaction. The logic is subtle yet decisive. Where a bad debt reflects income never collected, a refund reduces the very notion of income in the first place. Treating one as the other may inflate or understate profit in ways that ripple across tax returns.

Credits complicate matters further. They are not refunds, but adjustments—discounts applied after the fact, loyalty rewards redeemed against invoices, or foreign withholding taxes credited against domestic liabilities. Some credits reduce income directly, while others create deductible expenses. The classification hinges on context, and here jurisdictional quirks dominate. In Canada, certain sales credits must be netted against income; in the UK, credit notes often demand explicit reference to the original invoice for VAT compliance. In India, input tax credits are a labyrinth of eligibility, carry-forwards, and reconciliations with suppliers' filings. Misclassify a credit and a business may lose relief, misstate profit, or raise suspicion.

The underlying theme is one of discipline. Each unpaid invoice, each refund, each credit note is more than a transaction—it is a narrative. Why was the money not received? Why was it returned? Why was it reduced? The documentation is not busywork; it is evidence of integrity. Tax authorities do not expect perfection, but they do demand transparency. A ledger showing neat reconciliations, annotated with reasons and cross-referenced to correspondence, signals competence and honesty. A ledger riddled with gaps signals evasion, even if the errors were born of ignorance.

Case studies underline the stakes. A US freelancer once deducted bad debts without proof, only to face an audit that reclassified them as voluntary discounts. She owed tax on income never collected. A UK start-up applied customer refunds as expenses rather than contra-revenue, inflating turnover figures and jeopardising future VAT thresholds. A Canadian small business treated platform fee deductions as credits rather than expenses, muddling cost of sales and confusing investors. Each mistake was avoidable; each was born from treating paperwork as secondary to "real work."

Philosophically, the challenge reveals something deeper about commerce. Revenue is not an abstract number—it is a claim on trust. An unpaid invoice is a breach of that trust, a refund is a correction, and a credit is a recalibration. To record them accurately is to respect the fragile line between aspiration and reality. Founders often pride themselves on vision and growth, but in these small acts of accounting lies a truer test of stewardship: will they present their business as it is, not as they wish it to be?

The unanswered question hangs over every entrepreneur: how many ghosts linger in your books, masquerading as income that will never be realised? Until confronted, those ghosts distort not only financial statements but decision-making itself. For without clarity, how can a founder know whether growth is genuine, whether margins are healthy, or whether tax obligations are fair? The challenge is not merely to manage bad debts, refunds, and credits, but to master them—before they master you.

Chapter 4
Sales Tax, VAT, and the Line at the Till

It is one of the simplest gestures in commerce: a customer hands over money, a receipt prints, and both parties go on their way. Yet hidden within that transaction is a profound complexity that has toppled empires, triggered revolutions, and bankrupted otherwise thriving businesses. When American colonists dumped tea into Boston Harbour, they were not rebelling against the price of a beverage but against a sales tax imposed from afar. Centuries later, multinational corporations are still locked in disputes with tax authorities over how and where their value-added tax obligations arise. The line at the till may look ordinary, but it is one of the most contested borders in the history of trade.

For the modern founder, the paradox is sharper still. Income tax is painful but familiar—it takes from what you earn. Indirect taxes like VAT, GST, HST, or sales tax, however, are stranger creatures. They are not yours, though they pass through your hands. They accumulate in your account, looking deceptively like revenue, tempting you to spend what should have been set aside. The cruelest trap is that many entrepreneurs only discover the distinction when the first remittance deadline arrives, and the "extra" money has already been consumed by rent, wages, or advertising. Suddenly, a government claim arrives demanding thousands that no longer exist.

This mental separation—between what you collect and what you owe—is the cornerstone of solvency. Think of it less as tax and more as *trust money*. Each unit collected belongs not to the business but to the state, a deposit of civic duty momentarily resting in your account. The founder who recognises this truth avoids the common panic of mistaking borrowed funds for profit. The one who ignores it risks insolvency, even while sales are strong.

Complication does not end there. To whom, and how much, you owe is not simply a matter of national borders. It is shaped by thresholds and definitions—economic nexus rules in the United

States, distance-selling thresholds in the European Union, GST registration requirements in India, HST splits in Canada. A digital service sold from London to Berlin may trigger obligations different from those sold to Bangalore, even if the value and platform are identical. The "place of supply" is not a philosophical puzzle but a legal one, and misunderstanding it can lead to years of underpaid liabilities, interest charges, and backdated fines.

Even the invoice—often treated as dull paperwork—becomes a safeguard. A missing VAT ID, a wrongly stated rate, or an absent reverse-charge note can render a document non-compliant. The customer may be satisfied, the money exchanged, but the tax authority will not care. The small print, tedious as it seems, is in fact armour. It is what stands between an ordinary sale and a penalty notice, between trust and suspicion. The founder who learns to invoice correctly builds not just compliance, but credibility.

Cash flow, too, takes on a new character in this context. Unlike income tax, often paid annually or quarterly, sales taxes are frequently due monthly. They arrive with a drumbeat regularity, and they demand liquidity. Here lies the painful irony: businesses can go under not because they lack profit, but because they failed to park aside the money they were only ever holding in trust. A founder who adopts the discipline of a trust account, moving collected tax into a separate pool, transforms stress into confidence. Regular micro-reconciliations, performed like a ritual, preserve liquidity and allow the business to scale without hidden liabilities metastasising in the background.

This chapter steps into this contested space—not as a compendium of local quirks, but as a map of principles. It draws the bright line between income taxes and indirect taxes, between what is yours and what is not. It demystifies the thresholds that pull you into registration, the invoice requirements that insulate you from fines, and the cash flow practices that keep you solvent. Above all, it reframes indirect tax not as an enemy to be feared, but as a discipline that, once mastered, builds trust with customers, governments, and investors alike.

The line at the till is not merely a point of sale; it is the point at which responsibility transfers. The money in your hand may feel like yours, but it is already earmarked, its destiny predetermined. To recognise this early, and to act accordingly, is to shield your enterprise from the most avoidable of failures. The question that remains—one that every founder must face—is whether you will treat that line as a mere formality or as the sharp boundary it truly is.

What you collect vs what you owe

Imagine a small café in Toronto. At the till, a customer hands over ten dollars for a cappuccino and a slice of cake. The café owner rings it in, drops the note into the till, and moves on to the next customer. On the surface, it looks simple: a sale, a receipt, a bit of cash in the drawer. Yet buried in that ten-dollar note is a crucial distinction: only part of it belongs to the café. The rest is the government's money, entrusted to the owner for safekeeping until the tax authority calls it in. If the owner forgets this—if she spends that trust money on milk, wages, or even her own rent—she will find herself in a position that has bankrupted more than a few honest entrepreneurs: solvent in sales, but insolvent in obligations.

The paradox of indirect taxation is that it feels like revenue until it isn't. Unlike income tax, which arrives after profits have been tallied, sales tax, VAT, GST, or HST is collected upfront, embedded in every transaction. For the founder, this creates a dangerous mirage. The bank balance grows with each sale, yet a portion of that growth is already earmarked, claimed by the state. Those who mistake it for their own often discover the truth in the worst possible way—when a quarterly or monthly return comes due and there is no cash left to remit. The business may still be profitable on paper, but without the liquidity to pay its obligations, it teeters on the edge of collapse.

To prevent this trap, one must adopt a mental discipline: treat collected tax not as gain but as trust money. The term is not metaphorical. In law, these funds are held on trust for the government, and failure to pass them along is not a minor slip but a breach that can attract fines, penalties, and in some jurisdictions, even criminal liability. This is why separating what you collect from what you owe is not simply best practice—it is existential.

Consider the history of merchants in Renaissance Venice. Traders who failed to keep church tithes and civic levies distinct from their earnings were seen not merely as careless but as dishonest. The principle was clear: if you hold money on behalf of others, you are a steward, not an owner. The same logic applies to today's founders. Whether you run a one-person digital design studio or a multinational e-commerce operation, every sale that includes VAT or GST is a transaction in which you momentarily become an intermediary. The money passes through you, but it is not yours to spend.

And yet, the psychology of liquidity makes this discipline harder than it sounds. Bank accounts do not whisper which funds are yours and which are not. When a client pays £1,200 for a consulting engagement in London, with £200 of that being VAT, the deposit feels like a single sum. Unless the founder immediately siphons off that £200 into a separate account, the temptation is strong to view it as working capital. Advertising budgets are drawn, salaries are paid, subscriptions renewed—all from a pool that is quietly contaminated by trust money. The reckoning comes months later, when HMRC expects its £200, and the account balance has long since been drained.

The problem is amplified in the age of digital platforms. A Canadian app developer selling through a global marketplace may find that some platforms remit sales taxes on their behalf, while others deposit gross receipts, leaving it to the developer to sort out obligations. The opacity creates further risk of misclassification, leading to either underpayment or inadvertent double remittance. Without a strict internal rule that separates collected taxes from real revenue, the founder is left navigating in fog.

There are those who argue that this is simply a matter of better bookkeeping, of setting aside reserves and reconciling statements. But the deeper truth is philosophical: the line between what is yours and what is not must be internalised, not just recorded. Without that mental distinction, systems degrade. Employees learn bad habits. Founders rationalise away obligations. And soon, a business that looks healthy in sales metrics becomes fragile in its very foundations.

Practical defences do exist. One of the most effective is the trust account method: immediately moving collected tax into a separate bank account upon receipt. The account functions as a quarantine zone, insulating operational cash flow from liabilities. Another is the micro-reconciliation ritual: once a week, or even daily for high-volume businesses, matching recorded sales against expected tax liabilities and adjusting allocations. These practices may feel mundane, but they are the financial equivalent of hygiene—unseen, unglamorous, yet decisive in preventing illness.

The broader lesson is that collected taxes are not an administrative nuisance but a test of governance. Investors and partners often read compliance with VAT or sales tax regimes as a proxy for seriousness. A company that cannot distinguish between what it collects and what it owes is not just inviting regulatory penalties; it is signalling to stakeholders that it lacks the maturity to steward other people's money. And in truth, that is what this is about: stewardship. To handle trust money well is to prove the capacity for responsibility that underpins all durable commerce.

The founder who learns this lesson early gains more than compliance. They acquire peace of mind, the confidence that no sudden demand will appear to upend their operations. They build systems that scale, because the discipline of separating trust money applies whether a business has ten sales or ten thousand. The one who ignores it, by contrast, is like a sailor treating ballast as cargo—momentarily buoyant, but fatally unbalanced.

The question, then, is stark: do you view collected taxes as your money until the government takes it back, or as the government's money entrusted to you for safekeeping? The difference may appear semantic, but it is in fact existential. On that difference rests the solvency of your enterprise, the trust of your customers, and the resilience of your future. The till may click shut with every sale, but the story of that money is not finished when the drawer closes. It has further to go, and whether you let it travel safely is entirely in your hands.

Nexus, thresholds, and place of supply

In 2018, a small craft business in Minnesota found itself at the centre of a seismic shift in global taxation. The business sold handmade goods online, never imagining that sending parcels across state lines would expose it to tax obligations in places where it had never set foot. Yet the U.S. Supreme Court's *South Dakota v. Wayfair* decision declared that physical presence was no longer the threshold for sales tax. A seller could owe obligations purely through economic activity—simply by exceeding certain revenue or transaction counts. For countless small operators, the ruling felt like a trapdoor opening beneath them: suddenly, geography mattered in a way it never had before, and ignorance was no defence.

The story illustrates a paradox of modern commerce. The internet promised borderless trade, yet tax systems continue to draw sharp lines around jurisdictions. A transaction that looks identical from the seller's perspective—a customer clicking "buy" on a website—can trigger radically different obligations depending on where that customer happens to live. To understand why, we must reckon with three interlocking concepts: nexus, thresholds, and place of supply. Each one tells us not simply whether tax is due, but where it is due.

Nexus is the connective tissue between a business and a taxing authority. Once upon a time, it meant bricks and mortar: a shop in Paris, a warehouse in Mumbai, an office in Toronto. Today, the concept has stretched into the digital ether. Selling software subscriptions into Germany, or delivering online coaching sessions to clients in Australia, may create a nexus under local rules even if the business never crosses those borders physically. The principle is deceptively simple: if you benefit from access to a market, you may owe obligations to that market. The challenge lies in the thresholds—those measurable points at which "participation" becomes "obligation."

Thresholds operate as filters. Below them, a business may be exempt from registration, sparing micro-entrepreneurs from disproportionate burdens. Above them, obligations snap into place, often with startling abruptness. In the UK, for instance, surpassing the VAT registration threshold of £85,000 in taxable turnover obliges a business to register within thirty days. In the EU, cross-border digital services face a much lower bar: a €10,000 annual threshold across member states. Canada's GST/HST rules impose registration once a non-resident earns more than CAD 30,000 in a 12-month period. In India, thresholds vary by state and business type, but the Goods and Services Tax can attach with relatively modest turnover. These numbers may differ, but the pattern is universal: thresholds transform optional compliance into mandatory duty, and often with little grace period.

Consider the digital creator economy. A freelance designer in Lagos selling design templates on a U.S. platform may see deposits arrive net of platform fees. What looks like simple income conceals a labyrinth: does the platform collect and remit VAT on EU sales, or is the designer responsible? What happens when cumulative sales into one EU state cross the threshold? Without clarity on place of supply, the creator risks either overpaying (double remittance) or underpaying (exposure to penalties). For global platforms, these questions are baked into compliance departments. For individuals and small firms, they often surface only when an audit letter arrives.

Place of supply rules are the compass that determines which jurisdiction claims a transaction. For goods, the logic is usually tangible: where the customer takes delivery. For services—particularly digital ones—it becomes murkier. The EU's VAT rules, for instance, locate the supply of digital services at the customer's residence, not the seller's location. The same principle is echoed in many jurisdictions, reflecting a political commitment to tax consumption where it occurs. Yet exceptions abound. Some countries privilege the supplier's base for simplicity. Others apply hybrid tests involving billing address, IP location, or even SIM card data. To the founder, the effect is disorienting: the same webinar, streamed from a laptop in Singapore to clients worldwide, could trigger tax in ten different places under ten different logics.

This tension between local sovereignty and global commerce is not new. Medieval traders navigated overlapping levies from feudal lords as they crossed territories, each claiming a right to tolls and duties. Today's founder encounters the digital equivalent. Crossing the invisible borders of the internet does not erase those claims—it multiplies them. What makes this more urgent now is scale. A side project that once sold a few copies of an e-book can, overnight, reach thousands across continents. With scale comes visibility, and with visibility comes enforcement. Tax authorities, armed with data-sharing agreements and cross-border reporting standards, are increasingly able to track flows that once slipped beneath the radar.

How, then, should a founder approach nexus, thresholds, and place of supply without being paralysed? The first step is conceptual clarity: nexus tells you *if* a jurisdiction has a claim, thresholds tell you *when* that claim crystallises, and place of supply tells you *where* the tax is owed. The second step is operational discipline: track your sales by geography, monitor cumulative totals against known thresholds, and ensure invoices carry the right jurisdictional cues (from tax IDs to reverse charge notes). The third step is strategic humility: accept that you cannot master every local quirk alone. Thresholds will differ, interpretations will shift, and enforcement will tighten. The discipline lies in knowing when to escalate to specialist advice.

There is also a philosophical dimension here. These rules are not arbitrary: they reflect the ongoing negotiation between nation-states and the borderless economy. To comply is not merely to avoid penalties; it is to participate responsibly in the social contract of the markets you serve. Customers in Berlin, Mumbai, or Toronto are not just revenue streams—they are citizens of systems that fund infrastructure, courts, and protections that make commerce viable. Nexus is not just a bureaucratic hurdle; it is the legal recognition of interdependence.

Yet the future brims with unresolved tensions. As digital trade accelerates, will thresholds shrink to capture ever-smaller players? Will international treaties converge on uniform standards, or will fragmentation deepen? For now, the founder's challenge is practical: to distinguish revenue from responsibility, to track thresholds before they are crossed, and to map each sale onto a place of supply. But behind those practices lies a larger question: how long can a system designed around nation-states stretch to govern a marketplace that recognises none?

That question hangs unanswered, and perhaps unanswerable, but it is the space in which every modern entrepreneur operates. Nexus, thresholds, and place of supply are not abstractions—they are the ground rules of trust in the borderless bazaar we now call the internet. The founder who ignores them risks building on sand. The one who grasps them, however imperfectly, begins to build on something firmer.

Invoicing correctly: the small print that saves fines

In 2019, a thriving consultancy in London discovered that years of careful client work were being undone not by poor delivery, but by the layout of its invoices. A routine audit revealed missing VAT numbers, absent dates, and vague descriptions. The consequence was not academic: penalties were levied, input tax was disallowed for clients, and relationships strained under the weight of preventable errors. What felled them was not negligence in the boardroom or malpractice in the field, but oversight in the smallest of administrative details—the fine print that too often feels beneath the dignity of founders.

The paradox is striking. Businesses will obsess over their branding, their pitch decks, their social media presence. Yet the one document almost every client will see—the invoice—remains treated as an afterthought, a template downloaded in haste or a PDF cobbled together by a junior employee. But in the eyes of tax authorities, the invoice is not mere correspondence. It is the legal evidence of a transaction, the cornerstone of compliance, and often the very first artefact scrutinised when a file is opened. It is both receipt and declaration: proof that revenue was earned and that tax, if due, was correctly assessed.

Correct invoicing is therefore not a bureaucratic flourish but a safeguard. The required fields vary by jurisdiction but share a core logic. A valid invoice must state clearly who sold, who bought, what was supplied, when it was supplied, and at what rate of tax. Identification numbers anchor both parties in the system—VAT numbers in Europe, GST or HST numbers in Canada, GSTINs in India. Dates establish not just chronology but liability periods.

Descriptions prevent ambiguity, allowing auditors to classify goods and services without guesswork. Rates and totals show not just the financials but the method: whether VAT was applied, zero-rated, exempt, or subject to reverse charge. Each detail seems banal until its absence triggers scrutiny.

Take the reverse charge mechanism, a favourite of cross-border regulators. A German company hiring a UK freelancer post-Brexit may expect the invoice to carry the exact wording that VAT is shifted to the recipient. Omit that line, and both parties risk misreporting—the freelancer overstating their liability, the client losing deductibility. What appears to be a single missing sentence can, in practice, unravel thousands in penalties and administrative tangle. The invoice, in this sense, is not just a bill but a coded message, signalling to two tax systems how to interpret the same event.

One might imagine this is a problem only for large, complex firms. Yet the opposite is true. Smaller businesses face greater risk precisely because they lack layers of accounting staff and compliance checks. A yoga teacher in Toronto who issues receipts without HST registration numbers once past the CAD 30,000 threshold exposes herself to backdated obligations. An app developer in Bangalore who invoices without GSTIN may appear invisible to clients but becomes conspicuous to auditors. For these entrepreneurs, the invoice is not only paperwork but a shield. Correctly prepared, it demonstrates intent to comply, often softening the stance of authorities in the event of discrepancies elsewhere.

Technology has simplified the task without removing its gravity. Cloud platforms auto-populate fields, apply jurisdictional logic, and generate sequential invoice numbers. Yet automation can lull founders into false security. If the underlying settings are wrong—an outdated tax rate, a missing registration field—the system will faithfully replicate error at scale. This is why conscientious oversight remains indispensable. The founder must review periodically, ensuring templates evolve with regulation. Systems can carry, but vigilance steers.

Beyond compliance, correct invoicing carries a subtler power: it builds confidence at the point of sale. Clients interpret precise invoices as signals of professionalism. Investors read them as signs of governance. Even staff, watching how the business handles its obligations, internalise the culture of care. To dismiss invoices as trivial is to miss their symbolic weight: they are not just the paperwork of commerce but its public face of integrity.

There is also a moral undertone here. Taxes collected, rebates claimed, credits offset—all rest on the invoice as foundation. To issue them sloppily is to corrode the system of mutual trust that allows states to fund infrastructure and societies to accept commerce. To issue them correctly, by contrast, is to participate responsibly in that contract. The line items may look dull, but they are threads binding seller, buyer, and state in a shared transaction of accountability.

And yet, the landscape shifts constantly. What counts as valid today may evolve tomorrow with new directives, cross-border treaties, or digital reporting mandates. Countries are moving to e-invoicing systems that demand real-time uploads, eroding the gap between transaction and audit. For founders, this is both burden and opportunity: the burden of adapting, the opportunity to embed resilience early. The discipline of correct invoicing today prepares the business for a future in which every transaction is potentially visible, searchable, and enforceable in real time.

So the question becomes not simply, "Have I invoiced correctly?" but "Am I building a business where invoices will *always* be correct, regardless of scale or change?" It is not a task to be completed but a culture to be nurtured. For in the fine print lies not just the avoidance of fines, but the affirmation of trust—the quiet assurance that when the taxman calls, the business will stand upright, its records unshaken. And in that steadiness, a founder finds both compliance and credibility.

Filing cycles and cash management: A trust account method parks collected tax; monthly micro-reconciliations keep liquidity intact

In the aftermath of the 2008 financial crisis, one of the recurring stories in small business circles was not of market collapse or credit tightening, but of founders who failed because they spent money that was never theirs to begin with. Taxes collected at the till—VAT in Europe, sales tax in North America, GST in India—were mistakenly treated as income, absorbed into payroll, marketing, or expansion. When the filing deadline arrived, the coffers were bare. The authorities, unsympathetic to entrepreneurial optimism, demanded payment. What killed these businesses was not lack of demand, but lack of discipline in separating trust money from real revenue.

The paradox is sobering: a business can be profitable on paper and yet collapse under the weight of tax obligations. It is not uncommon to see companies with solid gross margins undone by mismanaged filing cycles. The difference between solvency and insolvency often lies not in strategy or sales but in whether a founder treats collected tax as an untouchable liability rather than a discretionary pool. This mental separation—reinforced through deliberate cash management—turns compliance from a reactive scramble into a stabilising rhythm.

Every tax system has its cadence. Some require monthly returns, others quarterly or annually. The periods seem innocuous, yet they dictate the flow of liquidity. A quarterly VAT return in the UK, for example, can mask three months of accumulated obligations that strike at once. A Canadian GST/HST filer may find that thresholds shift filing from annual to quarterly or even monthly, compressing the cycle of responsibility. In India, GST returns are monthly by default, with late fees compounding swiftly. The filing cycle is not simply a compliance calendar; it is a structural determinant of cash flow.

To manage this reality, seasoned entrepreneurs adopt the trust account method: every pound, dollar, or rupee of collected tax is transferred out of the operating account into a dedicated reserve, often within days of receipt. This is not an accounting trick but a psychological safeguard. By ring-fencing tax, founders prevent themselves from mistaking trust money for margin. The segregated funds serve as a quiet buffer, ready to be remitted, insulating operating liquidity from shocks. In effect, the business pays itself last but pays the taxman first, ensuring that survival is not contingent on end-of-quarter gymnastics.

Still, discipline cannot rely solely on quarterly reconciliations. Too much can go awry in three months: refunds issued, credits claimed, bad debts written off. A more resilient approach is monthly micro-reconciliation—brief but consistent reviews of inflows, outflows, and tax obligations. These thirty-minute sessions catch discrepancies before they metastasise: a misclassified sale here, a missing invoice there. Over time, they form not just a habit but a cadence, aligning financial practice with regulatory expectation. Like sharpening tools before use, these rituals ensure readiness long before inspection.

Consider the example of a mid-sized software platform selling subscriptions globally. Without monthly reconciliations, it may overlook VAT withheld at source by European platforms or GST collected automatically by marketplaces. At filing, the company could find itself double-reporting income or under-claiming credits. By contrast, the same company practising monthly reconciliation would record withheld amounts, offset them against obligations, and prevent overstated liabilities. The result is not just compliance but clarity—knowing precisely how much of the cash on hand truly belongs to the business.

The tension, of course, is between efficiency and rigour. Founders are time-poor, focused on growth. To them, carving out hours for reconciliation feels like overhead. Yet history shows that the true overhead is crisis management: scrambling for emergency credit to pay an unexpected tax bill, negotiating penalties, or defending an audit triggered by erratic filings. A disciplined filing cycle is not busywork but insurance, bought not with premiums but with foresight.

There is also a philosophical dimension. Taxes collected on behalf of the state are, in essence, trust money—temporarily held, never owned. To treat them otherwise is to violate the implicit contract between enterprise and society. This recognition reshapes the founder's mindset: filing cycles become not just deadlines but acts of stewardship. The business ceases to view tax as a predatory burden and begins to see itself as custodian of public funds, responsible for passing them on intact.

Yet even the most disciplined systems must contend with volatility. Exchange rates fluctuate, clients delay payments, refunds distort cash flow. The trust account method cushions these shocks but cannot eliminate them. The unresolved question remains: how does a founder design a system flexible enough to handle turbulence yet rigid enough to enforce discipline? Some resort to over-reserving, parking a margin above expected liability. Others adopt rolling forecasts, projecting obligations weeks ahead. All acknowledge the same truth: solvency is not secured at filing; it is secured in the months between, in the daily decisions to separate, reconcile, and respect the rhythm of the tax cycle.

Perhaps the most haunting question for any founder is this: if tomorrow the tax authority demanded full payment of your obligations, would you have the funds? The answer is rarely dictated by profitability or ambition, but by whether cash management practices respect the invisible line between trust and revenue. To blur it is to court fragility. To honour it is to build a business resilient enough to weather scrutiny, survive shocks, and, in the end, thrive with integrity.

Chapter 5
The Deduction Filter

In 1913, when the United States ratified its federal income tax, lawmakers confronted a familiar debate: what counts as a legitimate business expense? The phrase they settled on—"ordinary and necessary"—was as elegant as it was ambiguous. More than a century later, founders and freelancers from London to Bangalore still wrestle with the same puzzle. A conference ticket, a working lunch, a new laptop—are these fuel for the business or perks disguised as costs? The stakes are rarely academic. The difference between a defendable deduction and a disallowed one can mean the swing between liquidity and a painful letter from the tax authority.

The paradox is stark. Most entrepreneurs can close a sale with confidence or negotiate a contract with nuance, yet falter when asked the simplest of tax questions: is this deductible? Their uncertainty is not born of ignorance but of complexity. Tax codes expand into thousands of pages, swollen with exceptions, caveats, and footnotes. Attempting to memorise which categories "count" is a doomed exercise. The filter, not the list, is what matters. To survive audits and sleep soundly, one must internalise the principle: expenses must be ordinary, necessary, and demonstrable. This is the test that cuts through noise, transcending borders and jargon.

But clarity of principle is not enough; proof is the bridge between belief and defence. Here lies the second great trap. Many founders assume their recollection will suffice—"of course that flight was for business." Yet memory erodes, while auditors require evidence. A receipt without a note, or an invoice without a clear business purpose, quickly weakens under scrutiny. The history of tax disputes is littered with individuals who lost not because their expenses were improper, but because their substantiation was absent or sloppy. Documentation is the quiet currency of credibility, and systems that make its capture near-frictionless become as vital as the bank account itself.

The third layer of complexity arises not from the "whether" but the "how." Some costs are not deducted all at once but spread across years. A laptop, for instance, may be treated as a consumable in one jurisdiction and as a capital asset in another. Depreciation rules differ; small asset thresholds shift with inflation and policy. Timing becomes a strategic lever. To capitalise or to expense is not simply an accounting preference; it is a choice that can shape cash flow, investment timing, and even perceptions of profitability. Misjudged, it creates distortions. Understood, it becomes a tool.

And then come the grey zones—the categories that occupy folklore and fuel countless debates at café tables and coworking spaces. Meals: deductible in part, or not at all, depending on context and geography. Travel: obvious when linked to a client meeting, dubious when bundled with a family holiday. Education: justifiable when sharpening current skills, contentious when crossing into personal enrichment. Gifts: embraced in some regimes, tightly capped in others. These are the edges where temptation to stretch collides with the risk of grief. Here the Deduction Filter reveals its true value: it draws the line not where tax law happens to draw it this year, but where reason, defensibility, and prudence converge.

What is at stake is more than compliance. Deduction decisions shape culture. A founder who insists on discipline sends a message of stewardship, signalling that the business honours both its obligations and its long-term survival. Conversely, a cavalier approach corrodes trust within the team and erodes resilience. In this sense, the Deduction Filter is not merely a technical tool but a moral compass, teaching the entrepreneur to distinguish between what can be justified and what should be avoided.

As we step into this chapter, the path forward is not a catalogue of rules but a framework of discernment. We will ask not only what the law permits but what the records defend, not only what reduces today's bill but what strengthens tomorrow's solvency. The question for every founder is simple, yet profound: can you stand behind each expense when the lights are brightest and the questions sharpest? The answers will shape not just your tax return, but your confidence, your credibility, and the durability of the enterprise you are building.

Ordinary, necessary, and demonstrable: A three-part test replaces memorising lists

In the 1930s, a celebrated Broadway producer attempted to deduct the cost of champagne and flowers he lavished on actors, arguing that such gestures were vital to securing performances. The tax authority disagreed. Champagne, however charming, was not "ordinary." The case became an early example of a principle that now stretches across jurisdictions: expenses must be judged not by personal conviction, but by whether they pass a simple, enduring test.

Entrepreneurs today often find themselves in the same position, if less theatrical. The question is rarely whether the money was spent—bank statements make that obvious. The real question is whether the expense qualifies as deductible. Here, founders are tempted to search for lists: meals yes, gym memberships no; laptops yes, birthday parties no. But lists change. They are different in London and in Delhi, in Toronto and in New York. Worse, they are porous, full of exceptions that confuse more than they clarify. What endures is not the list but the filter: is the expense ordinary, necessary, and demonstrable?

Ordinary means it fits the pattern of what others in the same trade or profession would recognise as legitimate. An architect claiming drafting software is rarely challenged. A yoga teacher claiming night-vision binoculars would be. Ordinary is not universal, but contextual. What is expected in one field may be bizarre in another, and courts have consistently interpreted "ordinary" in that light. For a digital marketer, a subscription to analytics software is ordinary; for a carpenter, it is not. The word forces us to look outward—what would a reasonable peer in my line of work consider normal?

Necessary is narrower and more subtle. It does not mean indispensable; businesses operate with different levels of frugality or flair. Instead, it means the expense has a clear, direct connection to the generation of income. A freelancer buying a second monitor can argue necessity with ease—it directly supports productivity. A founder booking a luxury suite at a conference might struggle, unless they can show the suite was used demonstrably for hosting clients.

Tax systems do not reward extravagance disguised as business. Necessary asks: did this purchase support the trade, or was it a personal indulgence dressed up as strategy?

Demonstrable is the most pragmatic of the three, and the most often neglected. It insists that an expense, however ordinary and necessary, is worthless unless it can be proven. A flight ticket without an itinerary, a meal without a record of who attended and why, a subscription without an invoice—these fail the test. Auditors, after all, are not mind-readers. They rely on evidence, not memory. Here the line between legitimacy and loss is brutally clear: without substantiation, the deduction dissolves.

Consider a few cross-border illustrations. In the United States, meals are generally deductible at 50% when linked to business; in India, they are often treated with suspicion, allowed only in specific contexts such as staff welfare. In Canada, home office expenses must be proportionate to the space actually used; in the UK, flat-rate allowances simplify this but cap generosity. Yet across all of these regimes, the filter holds. A working meal with a client, noted and receipted, is defensible in any country; a vague claim for "food" is not. The principle travels even when the rules diverge.

This three-part test also guards against the temptation of *wishful deductions*. Entrepreneurs often reason backwards: "I want this to be deductible, therefore it must be." But tax codes are indifferent to desire. The filter imposes discipline. It creates a forward-looking question: *If challenged, could I explain this expense clearly, show its link to my trade, and produce evidence?* If the answer is no, the deduction is a liability, not an asset.

There is a philosophical elegance here. The tax system, often accused of being arbitrary and punitive, embeds in this test a kind of fairness. It does not require genius to interpret, only honesty and discipline. The producer's champagne failed because it was extravagant beyond the norms of the trade. The same principle protects a small business owner claiming the cost of the tools of their craft, even if those tools are invisible to outsiders. In this way, the filter mirrors an older truth: legitimacy comes not from assertion, but from the ability to defend one's choices before others.

The deeper challenge is behavioural. Lists lull us into passivity, while principles demand judgment. Judgment, in turn, requires time and reflection. The reward is resilience: once internalised, the three-part test travels with the entrepreneur across borders, industries, and evolving laws. It allows faster decisions, clearer conscience, and stronger defence. Ordinary, necessary, demonstrable: three words that, applied rigorously, transform deduction from a guessing game into a principled practice.

And yet, a question remains: if the test is so simple and durable, why do so many entrepreneurs still chase lists, loopholes, and legends? The answer lies not in law but in psychology—a topic to which we now turn, where clarity often collides with the allure of shortcuts.

Proof beats memory: substantiation that stands up

When the American gangster Al Capone was finally brought down in 1931, it wasn't for bootlegging, racketeering, or murder. It was for tax evasion. The government didn't need to prove every crime whispered about in Chicago speakeasies. They needed only records—bank deposits, ledgers, receipts—that showed income had been earned but not reported. What undid him was not the violence of his empire, but the paper trail he couldn't explain away.

The lesson is stark. Memory, however vivid, rarely stands up to scrutiny. In tax matters, the only narrative that counts is the one written down at the time. A founder who insists they "definitely" discussed business over dinner will find their recollection useless when an auditor asks for substantiation. Without a receipt, a note of purpose, or a contemporaneous log, the claim evaporates. Tax authorities do not reward good faith without evidence; they reward records that stand up under examination.

This insistence on proof has less to do with suspicion than with practicality. Administrations across the world—HMRC in the UK, the IRS in the US, the CRA in Canada, the CBDT in India—cannot divine intent. They rely on documentation because it creates verifiable fact. A receipt shows a sum was spent. A brief note—

"client lunch with Sarah James, discussed renewal terms"—shows why it was spent. A mileage log connects travel to trade. These are the building blocks of defensibility. Without them, even genuine business expenses collapse into personal anecdotes.

The paradox is that entrepreneurs are often deeply disciplined in their work but careless in their substantiation. They close deals, ship products, and deliver services with rigour, yet treat record-keeping as a distraction. The result is predictable: frantic searches for crumpled receipts at year-end, or worse, a tax bill inflated by disallowed expenses. Here, the line between profit and loss is not innovation or salesmanship, but the simple act of keeping track.

Fortunately, substantiation need not be burdensome. The old image of shoeboxes stuffed with paper receipts has been replaced by lightweight capture methods. A smartphone photo uploaded to cloud storage, a quick voice note attached to a digital expense entry, or automated feeds from bank accounts into accounting software—all create contemporaneous records without consuming hours. The discipline lies not in the complexity of the system but in the regularity of its use. Five seconds spent snapping a receipt is worth more than five hours reconstructing a forgotten trip months later.

Consider a freelancer driving to multiple client sites in a week. If they jot mileage in a notebook that same day, they can substantiate fuel costs with confidence. If they wait until year-end to reconstruct journeys, they risk errors, omissions, or suspicion. The same applies to subscriptions: a simple annual invoice stored in a dedicated folder can defend hundreds of pounds in deductions. Without it, the cost disappears into the fog of memory.

There is also a cultural difference worth noting. In the US, "substantiation" has become almost a term of art, shaped by court cases that hinge on receipts versus recollections. In the UK, HMRC is known for its insistence on "contemporaneous" records—logs made at the time, not after. Canadian authorities allow some estimates, but only if they are based on consistent record-keeping practices. Indian regulators have tightened enforcement, requiring detailed invoices and e-way bills for certain expenses. The global trend is unmistakable: documentation is no longer optional, it is foundational.

The philosophical insight here is that substantiation is not merely compliance; it is narrative control. Whoever writes the record at the time shapes the story later. Without receipts, the auditor's scepticism becomes the default story. With receipts and notes, the founder frames the narrative. Proof does not just beat memory—it supplants doubt with structure, replacing ambiguity with order. In a field as emotionally charged as tax, that shift brings peace of mind.

And yet, there is a lingering question. If the tools are so accessible and the stakes so high, why do so many founders still treat record-keeping as an afterthought? Perhaps because proof feels uncreative, even bureaucratic. But the entrepreneur who masters it gains an advantage subtler than innovation: the power to defend their work not just in markets, but before the state. The challenge, then, is not whether substantiation matters—it does—but whether the founder will choose to treat it as an integral act of business, rather than an inconvenient afterthought.

Capex vs expense: when the laptop is a tool or an asset

A laptop purchase is one of the most ordinary acts of modern business. Yet buried in that decision is one of the oldest puzzles of accounting: is this outlay an expense that dies in the year it is made, or an asset whose usefulness extends into the future? For the founder, the answer is not abstract but visceral. Classify it as an expense and it reduces this year's taxable profit, lightening the immediate tax bill. Treat it as capital expenditure, and only a portion—the depreciation—will count against income each year, stretching the benefit across the lifespan of the machine. The same object, the same price, but profoundly different effects on cash flow and timing.

This paradox—the dual identity of a single purchase—has haunted tax law for over a century. Early industrialists argued with revenue officers about whether a replacement part for a steam engine was "ordinary maintenance" or "new capital." Today, the arguments play out around laptops, software licences, and even website builds. Beneath the detail, however, lies a universal principle: expenses are consumed, assets endure. Tax systems the world over try to respect that difference, though each dresses it in its own rules and thresholds.

At its heart, capitalisation is a discipline of recognition. By recording the laptop as an asset, the books acknowledge that its value persists beyond a single year. Depreciation then spreads its cost, line by line, across the period of usefulness—three years in many regimes, five in others. The rationale is intellectual: profit in any year should be measured against the resources consumed in that year. If the laptop serves across multiple years, so too should its cost. This principle, rigorous as it sounds, becomes deeply practical when missteps distort reported profit. Expense everything too aggressively and the business looks weaker in its first years than it truly is. Capitalise too readily and cash flow strains under phantom profit while tax bills climb.

Governments attempt to resolve this tension with simplified rules for small businesses. The United States allows "Section 179 expensing," where assets up to a generous threshold can be written off immediately. The UK applies an "Annual Investment Allowance," enabling immediate deduction for many plant and machinery purchases. Canada offers accelerated depreciation under its Capital Cost Allowance. India provides block depreciation rates by asset class. The labels vary, but the intention is shared: to save smaller firms from bookkeeping contortions over modest assets, while retaining the capital-versus-expense distinction for larger outlays.

Consider a practical case. A consultant purchases a £1,200 laptop in the UK. If claimed under the Annual Investment Allowance, the full amount reduces taxable profit in year one. If instead treated under standard depreciation, perhaps only £400 per year is deductible. In the first scenario, cash is conserved when liquidity is most precious; in the second, profits look steadier across years. The tax authority recognises both treatments, but the choice shapes the entrepreneur's rhythm of survival.

This tension between immediate relief and longer-term smoothing recurs across contexts. A start-up in India may hesitate to capitalise small tools when cash is tight, preferring block depreciation rules that allow swifter recovery. A Canadian freelancer purchasing camera equipment might weigh the tax advantage of accelerated depreciation against the optics of more stable profit for lenders. In the United States, the choice between Section 179 and regular depreciation can shift the optics of profitability when courting investors. The same laptop, the same camera, the same server—each becomes a symbol of how timing choices echo far beyond bookkeeping.

Philosophically, the capex-versus-expense distinction is a reminder that accounting is not neutral. It imposes a story about time, endurance, and consumption. Treating something as an expense says: this died in the service of the present. Treating it as an asset says: this still lives, still serves, still has claim on future income. The founder must choose not only with an eye on compliance, but with an eye on narrative—what story do the books tell of this business's capacity to endure?

Yet herein lies the unresolved tension. Simpler regimes urge the small business to expense immediately for relief and ease. More traditional principles insist on capitalisation to reflect reality. The entrepreneur stands between them, pressed by the immediacy of cash flow and the longer horizon of credibility. Which to privilege? Which to delay? The choice will not be the same for every business, nor even for the same business at different stages. The only constant is that the laptop—the ordinary tool—remains the silent witness of that decision, its classification shaping the financial fate of the founder far more than its keyboard or screen ever could.

Grey zones: education, meals, travel, and gifts

The most dangerous tax deduction is not the one you forget to claim, but the one you claim too confidently. Auditors rarely argue with your rent or your utility bills. They reserve their sharpest questions for the ambiguous spaces—categories that feel personal as much as professional. Education, meals, travel, and gifts sit on this contested frontier. To the taxpayer, they often feel self-evidently tied to business survival. To the tax authority, they can look like lifestyle masquerading as necessity. The difference between the two is rarely in the headline expense; it lies in the fine grain of proof, proportion, and intent.

Consider a software developer who attends a week-long conference in Barcelona. The registration fee and technical workshops clearly advance her business knowledge. Yet she extends her stay for three extra days, dining by the beach and visiting museums. On her tax return, does she claim the entire hotel bill, or only the nights directly tied to the conference? Tax authorities the world over scrutinise such situations, aware that leisure often hides in the folds of learning. A misstep here can transform a legitimate professional investment into a red flag.

Education is perhaps the most emotionally charged of these categories. Few investments feel more rational than sharpening one's skills or entering new markets through knowledge. Yet the line between personal enrichment and business necessity is contested. A marketing consultant attending a short course on advanced analytics may be fully deductible in the United States, where the IRS allows expenses that "maintain or improve skills required in your trade." But if that same consultant enrols in a degree programme to pivot into a new field, deductions are denied. In the UK, the rule is even stricter: HMRC resists most education expenses unless they are directly required by the current business, rather than preparatory for a different one. The principle is consistent: what is *ordinary and necessary* in sustaining your trade is defendable; what is transformative or personal is not.

Meals follow a similar arc of tension. Breaking bread with clients or colleagues is as old as commerce itself. Yet how much of that sandwich or that dinner is truly business-related? The United States offers a cautious 50% deduction for meals tied to business discussions, recognising their role while curbing excess. Canada allows meals during travel or client meetings, but auditors demand precise records of who attended and why. In the UK, meals are generally deductible only when incurred during travel away from one's usual workplace. Across jurisdictions, the test is simple in spirit but complex in practice: was the meal genuinely for business, or was business invoked as an excuse for indulgence?

Travel stretches the paradox further. Flights to meet a client abroad are rarely disputed, but the temptation to blend business with leisure creates blurred edges. Some countries, such as Australia, require meticulous apportionment: the days spent in meetings are deductible, the holiday days are not. In the United States, foreign travel expenses are partly deductible depending on the proportion of business to personal activity. Even domestic travel can raise eyebrows if the destination happens to coincide with a family visit. The lesson is not to avoid travel, but to anticipate the sceptical questions an auditor will ask. Could you demonstrate, with records, that the journey was undertaken *because of business*, not merely *with business in mind?*

Gifts perhaps best embody the tension between human connection and regulatory suspicion. Businesses thrive on gestures of appreciation, yet tax systems fear abuse. A modest gift to a client—a bottle of wine, a book, or branded merchandise—may be allowed in the UK up to £50 per recipient per year, provided it carries the company logo or avoids luxury excess. In the United States, the deduction is capped at $25 per recipient, a figure that has barely shifted in decades. Canada denies deductions for most gifts unless tied to a promotional purpose. The principle is universal: generosity is respected when modest and business-focused, but penalised when lavish or personal.

What binds all these categories is not their outright prohibition, but their conditionality. They are not "yes" or "no" deductions; they are "yes, but…" The "but" often rests on substantiation: receipts, notes of purpose, itineraries, and clear separation of personal benefit. Without such anchors, even an entirely legitimate deduction may be disallowed. The irony is stark: a perfectly honest business expense can be lost to poor documentation, while a questionable claim can survive if supported by careful records. Proof, not intent, decides the outcome.

The philosophical thread here is revealing. Tax authorities do not merely regulate money; they regulate the stories people tell about their money. Was that meal a celebration or a negotiation? Was that trip an escape or an engagement? Was that gift personal gratitude or professional courtesy? The state asks not only what was spent, but *why*—and whether that "why" can withstand sceptical examination. This explains why these grey zones provoke such intensity: they touch the boundary between the private self and the professional self, the place where personal life shades into business life.

For the founder or freelancer, the safest path is rarely the most aggressive. Conservative claims—anchored in clearly defensible cores, carefully avoiding risky edges—may feel modest in the moment but build resilience over time. The alternative, chasing every arguable deduction, courts scrutiny that can undo years of careful work. The question is not just what can be claimed, but what can be confidently defended under audit.

And so the tension lingers. Education sharpens us, meals connect us, travel expands us, gifts humanise us. Yet the tax code views each through narrowed eyes, wary of personal pleasures cloaked as business costs. The entrepreneur must walk this line daily, claiming enough to reflect genuine business needs, yet cautious enough to avoid grief. The open question remains: in a world where work and life intertwine ever more closely, will tax codes evolve to recognise that reality—or will the boundary grow sharper still, forcing taxpayers to live in two separate stories of the same act?

Chapter 6
Home Office, Vehicles, and Mixed-Use Life

One of the defining features of modern work is that it refuses to stay neatly in its lane. The kitchen table becomes a boardroom. A personal car moonlights as a delivery fleet. Phones buzz with client calls and children's messages in the same hour. In this blurred reality, tax codes attempt to draw crisp lines—between business and private use, between deductible and non-deductible, between ordinary living and legitimate expense. For the founder, freelancer, or side-hustler, those lines are less an abstract debate than a daily reality. Misstep, and what felt like common sense in your life can collapse under audit.

The paradox is striking: the very tools that make flexible work possible—the spare room, the family car, the broadband connection—are also the ones most entangled in rules and restrictions. They are indispensable yet suspicious in the eyes of tax authorities, precisely because they serve dual purposes. The home office deduction has become a symbol of this paradox. For many, it represents an overdue recognition of the reality of modern work. For others, it has earned a reputation as a red flag, a claim that triggers scrutiny. The truth lies not in the myth but in the method: the way the deduction is calculated, documented, and defended determines whether it is a quiet ally or a source of grief.

Vehicles tell a similar story. Few assets carry such emotional weight—cars embody freedom, status, and personal identity. Yet they are also essential tools of commerce, whether for a plumber visiting clients or a consultant attending meetings. Tax authorities know this and respond with suspicion. The distinction between business mileage and a weekend trip is subtle in daily life but monumental in accounting. Here again, the burden falls not on intent but on record-keeping. Logs, consistent and credible, transform an expense from an assertion into an accepted fact.

Mixed-use life does not end at desks and steering wheels. It stretches into phones buzzing with both personal chats and client emergencies, into broadband that carries entertainment and work emails in equal measure, into software subscriptions that straddle convenience and necessity. Each of these is defensible when apportioned fairly, but each becomes hazardous when claimed carelessly. The habit of allocating clearly—whether by percentage, by time, or by function—creates stability. It allows deductions to survive contact with auditors, not merely with spreadsheets.

Property introduces its own layer of complexity. Renting a flat may allow a straightforward claim for a designated workspace—unless, as often overlooked, the landlord prohibits business use. Owning a home invites larger deductions in theory, yet exposes owners to restrictions on mortgage interest, potential capital gains complications, and regional quirks. Tax authorities here reveal a deeper philosophy: they resist allowing taxpayers to convert private shelter into a business subsidy without clear, narrow justification. The principle is not punitive; it is protective, aimed at preventing the gradual erosion of the boundary between personal life and taxable enterprise.

The scope of this chapter is therefore not just mechanical—though we will look closely at fixed versus simplified methods, at mileage logs, at monthly allocations, and at jurisdictional quirks. It is also conceptual. At its heart lies the tension between a lived truth—that modern tools serve both life and work—and a fiscal demand for separation. The reader will encounter examples that cross borders, showing how different systems wrestle with the same dilemmas, and how the conservative, well-documented approach tends to win.

Yet a question lingers beneath the calculations: in a world where work and life are increasingly inseparable, should tax codes adapt to acknowledge that reality more fully, or should individuals continue to perform the daily discipline of division? For now, the discipline is required, and it is within the control of each entrepreneur to choose whether it becomes a source of anxiety or of resilience. The lines may be blurred in life, but they need not be blurred in the books. The payoff is more than compliance—it is confidence, clarity, and the quiet assurance that one's mixed-use life can withstand even the closest inspection.

Home office: fixed vs simplified methods

The most contested square metres in modern taxation are often not in skyscraper offices or industrial warehouses, but in spare bedrooms, kitchen tables, and converted garages. A desk pushed against a wall can become the fulcrum of debate between a taxpayer and a revenue officer: is it business space or living space? A claim worth a few hundred pounds may hinge on whether a room is deemed "exclusively" used for work or not. The paradox is that what feels obvious in daily life—that a room functions as both study and dining room—is precisely what tax law resists. Authorities demand clarity, boundaries, and evidence, while human life flows in blurred lines.

Consider the early days of the pandemic, when millions scrambled to set up remote workspaces. Some spread files across the dining table. Others repurposed a child's bedroom. Governments offered relief in varying forms, yet the underlying principle remained: only defined, measurable space could translate into deductible expense. What was once a casual domestic adaptation became a fiscal classification problem. In this, the home office deduction is less about the furniture or the walls than about the narrative you can defend: is this space *demonstrably* part of your business infrastructure, or merely a convenience?

Two primary approaches dominate worldwide practice. The first is the *area-based method*—meticulously calculating the proportion of your home used for work, often based on square footage or room count. It promises precision but demands substantiation: floor plans, photos, or at least a reasoned calculation kept on record. This method appeals to those with dedicated space—a converted loft office, a garden studio, or a spare bedroom used exclusively for business. Yet it also invites scrutiny, because tax authorities know the temptation to inflate proportions. A claim that a third of one's flat is "office" in central London, for instance, may draw questions unless backed by unambiguous evidence.

The second is the *simplified method.* Many jurisdictions, recognising both the administrative burden and the inevitable disputes, have introduced fixed-rate allowances. In the UK, HMRC permits a flat monthly claim depending on hours worked from home, regardless of actual area. In the United States, the IRS offers a simplified option of a set dollar rate per square foot up to a capped area. Canada and India followed similar paths during the pandemic, introducing streamlined formulas. These methods sacrifice some precision but reward compliance with predictability and ease. They are designed to remove ambiguity, reduce disputes, and lower the administrative barrier for small businesses and freelancers.

The choice between these two approaches is not merely mechanical. It reflects a trade-off between precision and peace of mind, between maximising potential deduction and minimising risk. The area-based method may yield higher claims if one's home is particularly business-oriented, but it requires a readiness to defend every assumption. The simplified method, by contrast, is conservative but bulletproof, offering the reassurance that authorities are unlikely to challenge what they themselves prescribed. For many, especially early in their business life, this certainty is worth more than the incremental tax saving.

Documentation is the quiet determinant of outcome. A floor-plan sketch with areas shaded, date-stamped photographs of a room arranged as an office, utility bills apportioned with clear reasoning—all these form the defensible trail that separates a legitimate deduction from a contested one. Where the simplified method is chosen, the discipline is lighter but not absent: a log of hours or weeks worked from home can prevent doubts later. The underlying principle is consistency: whatever method is chosen, it must be applied in the same way year after year, not opportunistically varied to optimise tax in hindsight.

International contrasts sharpen the picture. In Germany, the home office deduction is traditionally restrictive: only rooms used exclusively and permanently for business are eligible. By contrast, in the United States, the simplified method has softened long-standing suspicion of home office claims, though the exclusive-use test remains. In India, clarity is still evolving, with many deductions treated on a case-by-case basis, making contemporaneous documentation all the more critical. These differences illustrate a common tension: governments acknowledge the reality of remote work but remain wary of its potential as a loophole.

Beyond mechanics lies a philosophical question: what does it mean to transform private space into business infrastructure? For entrepreneurs, the home office is not a luxury but a necessity, yet the very intimacy of the claim invites distrust. This is why conservative, unambiguous evidence matters: it signals to the authorities that one respects the boundary between personal and business, even when life does not. The act of photographing a workspace or mapping a floor plan is not bureaucracy for its own sake—it is a ritual of clarity, a way of aligning messy lived reality with the tidy boxes of tax forms.

The unresolved tension is whether these methods will continue to suffice as the boundary between home and office dissolves further. With hybrid work entrenched and digital tools redefining where business "happens," how long can a binary choice between area-based and simplified methods capture the reality? Perhaps future systems will integrate time, mobility, and digital presence as readily as they now measure square metres. Until then, the conservative path—documenting clearly, choosing methods wisely, and prioritising defensibility—remains the foundation. The numbers claimed matter less than the story they tell, and a story told with clarity is one that endures.

Vehicle use: logs that don't ruin your week

There is a familiar groan that echoes across small businesses every tax season: the discovery that vehicle use must be justified, not guessed. Somewhere in the glove compartment sits a crumpled pile of petrol receipts, maintenance invoices, and perhaps a half-filled notebook of mileage entries abandoned months earlier. The paradox is stark—cars are among the most tangible, visible assets a business uses, yet the tax claim attached to them can dissolve instantly without credible records. The physical presence of the vehicle counts for nothing if the paper trail falters.

Governments know this. From the IRS in the United States to HMRC in the UK, tax authorities have long considered vehicle deductions a high-risk category. They see the temptation: blurring the line between school runs and client visits, or calling a family holiday a "conference trip." This scrutiny means the standard of evidence is higher, and the discipline required sharper, than in many other expense areas. Yet the solution need not be bureaucratic agony. What matters is not perfection but consistency—habits that create a defensible picture without consuming your week.

The two dominant approaches to claiming vehicle expenses reflect this balance between accuracy and simplicity. The *mileage method* converts business distance travelled into a deduction at a fixed per-mile or per-kilometre rate. It is clean, predictable, and often generous for those who drive modest distances in fuel-efficient cars. The *actual-cost method*, by contrast, apportions all vehicle expenses—fuel, insurance, repairs, depreciation—between personal and business use, usually based on mileage percentages. This method can yield higher deductions when cars are heavily used for business or costly to run, but it also requires careful record-keeping and often more scrutiny.

Take an example. A consultant in Toronto logs 10,000 kilometres in a year, half of which are for client visits. Under Canada's mileage rate system, they can deduct 5,000 kilometres multiplied by the government-set per-kilometre rate, with no need to calculate actual fuel or depreciation. If they chose the actual-cost method, they would tally fuel receipts, insurance premiums, car loan interest, maintenance, and depreciation, then allocate 50% as business. Both methods are valid, but each leads to different outcomes depending on the vehicle, the travel, and the records maintained.

The friction lies in logging. A mileage-based claim demands a record of trips—start and end points, kilometres travelled, and business purpose. The traditional image of keeping a paper logbook in the car is enough to deter many from even trying. Yet modern tools, from smartphone apps to GPS-enabled trackers, have turned this burden into a background task. Automatic logging apps can record every journey, leaving the user to categorise trips weekly or monthly, a task of minutes rather than hours. Even without technology, a disciplined habit of noting journeys in a diary or spreadsheet at the end of each day creates a reliable trail.

The actual-cost method requires different discipline: retaining receipts, invoices, and insurance documents, then apportioning expenses by a defensible percentage of business use. Here too, consistency matters more than exactitude. Authorities are not demanding forensic certainty about every litre of petrol used for personal errands versus business trips. What they require is a method applied consistently, year after year, with numbers that can be tied back to contemporaneous records. A 60/40 split declared for three years with logs and receipts is far more defensible than a fluctuating claim that seems optimised for tax savings alone.

International variations sharpen these choices. In the United States, the IRS allows switching between mileage and actual-cost methods, but only under strict conditions—changing too frequently raises suspicion. In the UK, HMRC's simplified mileage allowance eliminates depreciation claims, but its predictability makes it popular with sole traders. Germany, by contrast, often leans heavily on actual-cost methods, requiring meticulous receipts but allowing generous depreciation. Each system balances administrative burden against potential abuse, but all share one expectation: without records, no deduction stands.

Behind the mechanics lies a deeper lesson: the value of discipline over intensity. Many entrepreneurs wait until year-end to reconstruct their driving history, a futile exercise of guesswork and stress. A few minutes weekly—scanning receipts into a folder, categorising mileage logs—removes the need for such reconstruction and builds a record that is both credible and calming. The aim is not to capture perfection but to prevent ambiguity. Revenue authorities are more lenient towards a business owner who shows consistent, modest logging than towards one who presents nothing and improvises when challenged.

There is also a psychological angle. Vehicle deductions are often inflated not out of malice but out of self-deception. Business owners convince themselves that a greater proportion of their driving is work-related than reality supports. Regular logging confronts this bias. By tracking in real time, the truth is recorded before memory has a chance to revise. The logbook, whether paper or digital, becomes not just a tax defence but a mirror of how business activity actually shapes daily movement.

The tension unresolved is whether vehicle deductions will remain a major category as the world shifts. With the rise of remote work, fewer client visits occur by car. Electric vehicles complicate fuel-based assumptions, while ride-sharing and rentals blur ownership models. Tax codes, often written with combustion engines and commuting in mind, lag behind these changes. For now, the best defence remains the same: adopt a method, log consistently, and present a clear story. The car itself cannot speak, but your records can. And if they do, they should sound calm, coherent, and believable.

Phones, internet, and subscriptions: Mixed-use items are allocated fairly with monthly rules to reduce year-end guesswork. Stable deductions emerge without drama

There is a quiet irony at the heart of modern business: the devices and connections that make professional life possible are the same ones that blur its edges. The phone in your pocket fields client calls and personal chats in the same breath. The broadband bill pays equally for a board meeting conducted over Zoom and an evening of streaming films. Even subscriptions—software, digital news, cloud storage—often serve a dual role, straddling professional necessity and personal convenience. The very tools that dissolve boundaries between work and life complicate the financial lines that tax systems insist must be drawn.

This tension becomes most apparent at year-end, when founders and freelancers alike attempt to reconstruct a year's worth of "business use." Memories prove unreliable. Did half your mobile data really go to conference calls, or was it a third? Was that streaming platform used only for relaxation, or did its documentaries occasionally inform your work? When estimates replace records, deductions wobble from defensible to dubious. Yet it need not be this way. A steady, month-by-month allocation method transforms messy guesswork into stable, defensible claims—without requiring the obsessive tracking of every phone call or gigabyte consumed.

At the centre is a principle as old as accounting itself: fairness. Authorities expect that if a cost is split between personal and business use, the allocation reflects reality and can be explained without hesitation. In practice, this means setting a percentage once—based on logs, bills, or reasoned estimates—and then applying it consistently. A self-employed architect, for example, who analyses her phone usage for a representative month and finds 70% of calls are business-related can apply that proportion throughout the year. She need not record every conversation, only keep the initial analysis as a baseline. The virtue lies in reasonableness, not precision.

Consider the internet bill, often the most significant shared utility in a home office. Few tax authorities expect individuals to split broadband usage by the hour or megabyte. Instead, they look for consistent allocation tied to professional necessity. A freelance writer who spends weekdays online researching and submitting work can justify allocating 60% of monthly costs to the business, even though family members also use the connection in evenings. A conservative approach may choose 50% to avoid challenge. The key is documentation: keeping copies of invoices and, ideally, a brief note explaining the chosen percentage and rationale.

Subscriptions illustrate another layer of complexity. Some are unequivocally professional: accounting software, design tools, cloud storage for client files. Others, like general news outlets or video platforms, straddle personal and professional worlds. Here, defensibility depends on clarity. If the subscription is used materially in business—say, an academic citing articles from a paid journal, or a podcaster sourcing audio from a licensed library—the expense can be claimed proportionally. But if the business link is tenuous, the safe course is exclusion. Chasing the last marginal deduction often creates more audit risk than tax saving.

International differences sharpen the need for care. In the UK, HMRC guidance on phone and internet expenses explicitly acknowledges apportionment between business and personal use, but expects claims to be "just and reasonable." In the US, the IRS similarly allows mixed-use deductions but insists on records to support allocations, with a particular eye on excessive or all-inclusive claims. In Canada and Australia, authorities take a broadly similar stance—allocate fairly, keep records, avoid overreach. None require impossible precision; all expect transparency.

Technology itself offers solutions. Mobile phone bills increasingly separate call logs, data usage, and even app-level consumption. Screenshots of these summaries, taken periodically, provide defensible evidence of usage proportions without requiring exhaustive tracking. Internet routers sometimes record device-level usage, making it possible to distinguish work computers from family tablets. Subscription services often issue detailed invoices, which can be annotated with brief notes of business use. In each case, light but regular capture beats heavy, last-minute reconstruction.

Beyond compliance, there is a philosophical dimension worth pausing on. Mixed-use costs reflect the reality that modern work is not neatly bounded. The smartphone is at once a professional lifeline and a personal appendage. Broadband sustains both commerce and leisure. To allocate fairly is not merely to satisfy tax codes but to acknowledge this duality with honesty. It requires resisting the temptation to tilt every ambiguity in favour of the business, while also resisting the opposite temptation of under-claiming out of fear. The discipline lies in balance: neither inflated nor timid, but grounded.

Monthly rules bring this balance to life. By reviewing bills and usage regularly—twelve times a year rather than once—business owners build stability into their deductions. This prevents the familiar panic of December, when vague recollections stand in for evidence. It also smooths cash flow, as set-aside amounts for tax are based on realistic expense claims, not end-of-year surprises. Over time, the practice becomes second nature, part of the rhythm of business rather than an exceptional chore.

What remains unresolved, however, is how these allocations will evolve as technology itself shifts. With bundled services, family plans, and integrated platforms, distinguishing business from personal may grow harder. Will tax systems adapt with more simplified allowances, or will they continue to demand proportioning of ever more entangled costs? For now, the soundest path is pragmatic: choose a reasonable split, document it lightly but clearly, and repeat it consistently. The phone in your pocket and the connection in your home may blur boundaries in daily life, but in your accounts, they should draw clean, defensible lines.

Renting vs owning: edges and exclusions

Imagine a freelance consultant in Berlin, working from a rented flat. Her landlord has no objection to her laying out a desk in the spare bedroom, but would bristle if she advertised the address as her official office. Meanwhile, a tech founder in Toronto claims part of his mortgage interest against his business income, but finds that capital gains tax rules later claw back benefits when he sells the property. The same act—using a home for business—plays out differently depending on whether one rents or owns, and those differences ripple through obligations, entitlements, and long-term consequences.

The paradox is that a home office feels universal in practice yet deeply particular in law. Tax authorities across jurisdictions recognise the blurred reality of mixed-use space, but they draw their lines with different pens. For tenants, the issue is rarely the apportionment of rent—straightforward enough when measured by square metres—but whether the lease permits such use at all. A landlord's consent, explicit or implied, becomes the hidden hinge. For owners, the complication lies not in permission but in consequences. Mortgage interest relief, depreciation claims, or local property tax offsets may be allowed, but they often come tied with exclusions that limit future benefits or generate liabilities at sale.

The distinction matters most in audit. A tenant who cannot show landlord consent risks disallowance even if their apportionment is mathematically impeccable. Tax authorities do not want to see deductions built on shaky legal ground. Conversely, an owner who has aggressively claimed every possible expense may be surprised to find their future capital gain partly taxable, the tax office arguing that part of the property was "not a principal residence" but a business asset. What looks like a prudent deduction today may prove an expensive adjustment years later.

Consider the UK. Renters may deduct the proportion of rent and utilities used for business, provided the space is genuinely and regularly dedicated to work. But if the lease prohibits sub-letting or commercial use, the claim becomes vulnerable. Owners can claim a portion of mortgage interest and council tax, but if the workspace is deemed "exclusive"—a room used only for business—the future sale may trigger partial capital gains tax. The system nudges taxpayers towards moderation: flexible use avoids both immediate denial and long-term penalties.

In the United States, the IRS enforces a strict "exclusive and regular use" test for the home office deduction. For renters, this is mainly a matter of floor area, with no need to involve the landlord unless lease terms forbid it. For owners, the deduction allows mortgage interest and depreciation, but the depreciation element creates a permanent record. Upon selling, that portion of depreciation is recaptured as taxable income, even if the house itself would otherwise be exempt under the principal residence rules. What feels like a win in year one can carry a sting in year ten.

Canada offers another lens. Tenants apportion rent, insurance, and utilities, but must stop short of exaggeration. Owners claim mortgage interest and property taxes, but capital cost allowance—depreciation—is optional and carries the same trap as in the US: claiming it today reduces shelter from capital gains tomorrow. The Canada Revenue Agency openly advises caution, signalling that conservative claims are both safer and more sustainable.

Australia, meanwhile, distinguishes between "occupancy expenses" (rent, mortgage interest, property rates) and "running expenses" (utilities, internet). Tenants can deduct both if they have a dedicated workspace. Homeowners face a choice: claim occupancy expenses and risk part of the property being treated as a taxable business asset, or stick to running expenses only and preserve full exemption when selling. Again, the hidden trade-off is not in the annual return but in the lifetime trajectory of ownership.

Behind these technicalities lies a larger question: how should the tax system treat the blurred edges of modern life? A kitchen table doubling as a workstation in Milan is hardly a commercial enterprise. Yet tax law cannot simply ignore it, for to do so would invite abuse by those with genuine home offices. Nor can it fully embrace it, for that risks distorting the housing market and penalising homeowners on sale. The result is a patchwork of cautious allowances, each jurisdiction balancing encouragement with restraint.

Practical navigation begins with clarity. Tenants should check leases for restrictions on business use and, if necessary, request written consent. Even a short email from a landlord can transform a fragile claim into a robust one. Owners should think not only about this year's return but about their longer-term plans. If selling the property is foreseeable, limiting deductions now may preserve a larger gain later. Documentation is again the safeguard: floor plans annotated with the office area, records of bills, and contemporaneous notes of business use.

The temptation, especially in start-up years, is to maximise deductions when cash is tight. Yet history shows that overreach often backfires. Tax authorities do not need to prove fraud; they need only show inconsistency, lack of permission, or disregard for exclusions. By contrast, a restrained, well-documented approach often survives scrutiny with little dispute. The most resilient strategy is not to squeeze every possible deduction but to build a pattern of claims that can be defended calmly and explained simply.

The deeper philosophical tension remains: our homes are increasingly sites of production as well as consumption, yet tax codes still cling to binary categories of personal and business. Renting and owning only sharpen the distinction, forcing individuals into choices that can have consequences years down the line. Will future reforms recognise the hybridity of modern life, or will taxpayers continue to navigate edges and exclusions designed for an earlier era? For now, the discipline lies in reading not only the tax code but the fine print of leases and the long arc of ownership—balancing today's savings against tomorrow's risks.

Chapter 7
Estimated Taxes and the Art of No Surprises

It is one of the most peculiar rites of modern work: the professional who appears outwardly successful, bills paid, projects thriving, only to find themselves hollowed by a sudden tax bill that feels like it has arrived out of nowhere. In that moment, the past year's triumphs collapse into panic. The income was real, but the cash is gone. What was meant to be reinvested in the business or tucked aside for savings must instead be scraped together in haste to satisfy the state. Few forces remind us more sharply of the difference between earned and kept.

The irony is that the system was designed to prevent exactly this. The practice of paying taxes as you go—through quarterly estimates for the self-employed, or payroll withholding for employees—was born not out of malice but necessity. In wartime economies of the twentieth century, governments discovered that waiting until year's end to collect was disastrous for both revenue stability and citizen solvency. A pay-as-you-go structure was introduced to spread the burden evenly, to keep governments funded, and to keep individuals from being crushed by a single, unmanageable bill. What began as an emergency measure became a permanent fixture of fiscal life across much of the world.

And yet, despite its logic, estimated tax remains one of the most resented obligations for entrepreneurs and professionals outside payroll systems. It feels arbitrary, even punitive. Why should one prepay on money that has barely cooled in the bank account? Why should compliance depend not on one tidy deadline but on a rhythm of instalments that must be remembered, calculated, and met? The answer lies partly in psychology. Human beings are not built to carve out slices of prosperity in advance. Left alone, most will consume or reinvest in the present, hoping vaguely that the future will sort itself out. The quarterly cycle forces discipline where instinct falters.

To understand this obligation fully is to see its fairness. The quarterly payment is not an extra tax but simply the same income tax spread across time. Safe harbour rules—minimum payments based on the prior year's liability—exist not to trap taxpayers but to create certainty. They provide a floor: meet these, and penalties fall away, even if income rises beyond expectation. In this sense, estimated taxes are a compact between state and citizen, a deal that trades precision for peace of mind. You may underpay slightly or overpay slightly, but you are spared the agony of surprise.

Two philosophies guide calculation. One looks backward, pegging payments to the last known year. This suits those whose income grows steadily or modestly; it is predictable, and it locks in safe harbour protection. The other looks forward, attempting to match payments to the current year's trajectory. This is riskier but more responsive, sparing the entrepreneur from lending too much to the treasury when revenues are surging or sagging. Each method carries a philosophy of time: do you prefer the stability of the past, or the agility of the present? The choice is less about arithmetic than about temperament.

Across borders, the labels change but the logic repeats. In the United States, Form 1040-ES structures quarterly payments, often through online portals. In the United Kingdom, the "payment on account" system requires two instalments in January and July, with a balancing payment at year-end. Canada expects quarterly instalments in March, June, September, and December, unless payroll or withholdings already cover the liability. India asks for advance tax in four tranches across the financial year, with penalties for those who underpay by more than 10 per cent. The rhythms differ, but the principle is identical: reduce the shock, keep the flow steady.

Still, the difficulty is not knowing *what* to do but doing it consistently. The self-employed founder who leaves tax payments to memory will inevitably miss a due date or overestimate their cash flexibility. The wiser ones automate: each week or month, a fixed percentage of income is swept into a separate account reserved for tax. It is money already spoken for, held in trust until the instalments are due. Modern banking apps and accounting software make this a trivial task, but the discipline lies not in the tool but in the ritual. By embedding estimated taxes into the rhythm of financial life, the system becomes less an ordeal and more an unconscious habit.

The deeper lesson here extends beyond tax. Estimated payments embody a broader truth about resilience: shocks are cushioned not by brilliance but by foresight. The entrepreneur who resists quarterly planning may feel freer in the moment but will be more fragile when obligations crystallise. The one who embraces the routine finds that solvency and serenity go hand in hand. What seems like bureaucratic busywork is, in reality, a structure for freedom—the freedom to focus on work and growth without the constant dread of a lurking bill.

But one question lingers. If pay-as-you-go systems were meant to eliminate surprises, why do so many still feel ambushed when deadlines loom? Perhaps the issue lies not in the mechanics but in our relationship to time, to discipline, and to the trade-offs between present consumption and future security. The quarterly cycle is not just about tax—it is about learning to live with the future as a constant presence. Whether we embrace it as habit or fight it as burden may reveal more about us than about the system itself.

Why quarterly payments exist

Imagine the farmer at harvest. He brings in his crops once a year, sells them, and only then holds the means to pay his obligations. For centuries, taxation mirrored this rhythm: a lump sum demanded after income was gathered, often in grain, coin, or livestock. But as economies industrialised, populations urbanised, and governments shouldered the burdens of war and welfare, such annual reckoning became untenable. The state could not wait twelve months for its revenues, nor could citizens absorb the shock of a massive bill without warning. Out of this tension was born the pay-as-you-go model—one of the most quietly revolutionary shifts in public finance.

The paradox is striking: quarterly tax payments, which feel like a burden of constant vigilance, were introduced to reduce pressure, not increase it. They are designed to prevent ruinous surprises.

During the Second World War, the United States adopted withholding at source to fund its war effort, spreading the burden across each payday rather than demanding a single large sum later. Britain, under similar strains, refined its "Pay As You Earn" system to ensure both solvency and fairness. Canada, India, and many other countries followed variations of this model. The intent was pragmatic: a steady flow of cash for the government and a gentler, more predictable obligation for the taxpayer.

Yet the human reaction to quarterly obligations remains conflicted. People bristle at writing cheques four times a year, while employees hardly notice deductions spread across pay slips. This contrast exposes a deep psychological truth: steady, invisible obligations are tolerated, while visible lump sums—no matter how fair in theory—provoke resistance. Quarterly estimated tax is not punishment for the self-employed; it is an attempt to mimic the smoothing effect of payroll withholding, to align tax with income as it arises. The frustration lies not in the principle but in its visibility.

To see why this structure matters, one must grasp the notion of *safe harbours*. In tax law, these are not nautical metaphors but real thresholds: pay a minimum amount, often based on the previous year's liability, and you are shielded from penalties even if your income surges. In the United States, for instance, paying 100–110 per cent of last year's tax generally protects against underpayment fines. Similar systems exist in the UK and Canada, with their own mechanics. These rules reduce uncertainty. You may still owe a balancing payment, but you will not be punished for failing to predict the future. Quarterly payments, in this light, are not about precision—they are about security.

Consider two entrepreneurs. One ignores the quarterly system, spends freely through the year, and arrives at filing season staring at a tax bill equal to several months of income. Panic ensues, debts are juggled, and stress corrodes the work itself. The other makes steady instalments, perhaps even overshooting slightly. At year's end, she finds her liability already met—or a modest refund waiting. Same income, same tax rate, but utterly different lived experience. The discipline of pay-as-you-go transforms tax from a lurking ambush into a manageable routine.

There is also a philosophical angle. Quarterly payments embody a social contract: citizens fund the state continuously, not retroactively. Roads are paved, hospitals staffed, and courts maintained month by month, not in an annual burst. To align funding with service is to acknowledge that society's machinery does not pause between harvests. Just as a household budget falters if rent is left until year's end, so too would public finance collapse without steady inflows. Quarterly taxes, then, are not merely administrative—they are a mirror of collective life.

But history leaves us with a tension. The very system designed to protect against shocks now generates resentment because it is conspicuous. Employees rarely think of their tax as "quarterly" or "annual"—they see a net figure on their payslip. The self-employed, however, must actively calculate, transfer, and pay, forced to engage with the process. This visibility, while painful, brings with it a certain clarity. The entrepreneur who manages quarterly tax effectively tends also to manage cash flow with greater foresight, learning to separate "available" cash from "spoken-for" cash. The pain of quarterly cheques may sharpen the very discipline that ensures survival.

The lesson is twofold. Quarterly payments exist because governments cannot wait, and citizens cannot safely delay. They are a structure born of necessity, hardened by war, and preserved by the logic of fairness. They represent not extra tax, but earlier tax—an alignment of payment with income that prevents collapse. And yet, even knowing this, resistance remains. Perhaps the unresolved question is this: can a system designed to ease the burden ever feel light, when it requires us to confront, four times a year, the uncomfortable reality of our obligations?

That question—whether discipline can be reconciled with ease—lingers beyond tax. It touches on how societies distribute burdens, how individuals plan for the future, and how we navigate the eternal conflict between present enjoyment and deferred responsibility. The quarterly cycle is only one answer, imperfect and contested, to that larger human puzzle.

How to calculate a sane estimate

There is a moment every freelancer, entrepreneur, or small business owner dreads: sitting before a spreadsheet, staring at income figures that feel both promising and precarious, and asking, *how much of this is truly mine to spend?* The paradox is cruel. To misjudge upwards—hoarding too much for tax—can starve your business of the fuel it needs to grow. To misjudge downwards—spending too freely—can turn tax season into a crisis. Somewhere between paralysis and recklessness lies the craft of calculating a *sane estimate.*

Consider the case of a graphic designer who left salaried employment to go independent. In her first year, she did brilliantly: £75,000 in gross revenue, with expenses that left her £55,000 in taxable profit. But she made one error. Each time a client paid her, she treated the money as spendable. Holidays, software, even a new car—all funded from a pool she believed was "hers." When the tax authority's bill arrived—nearly £15,000—her savings evaporated in weeks, leaving her scrambling. Her work was profitable, but her cash flow was broken. It was not ignorance of tax law that undid her; it was the absence of a disciplined method for estimating and setting aside what was already spoken for.

At its heart, the problem is philosophical as much as it is numerical: how do you live fully in the present while honouring obligations that are invisible until they fall due? The answer lies not in perfect foresight but in *sufficient structure.* Two broad methods—anchored in history and practice—provide that structure: the last-year method and the live-year method. Each suits a different kind of business rhythm.

The last-year method is the safer harbour. It looks backwards, not forwards. Take your prior year's tax bill, divide it into four, and pay that much in estimated instalments. Tax systems in the United States, the UK, Canada, and elsewhere enshrine this principle in their "safe harbour" rules. In the US, for example, paying 100 per cent of last year's liability (or 110 per cent if your income is high) guarantees freedom from underpayment penalties, even if your income doubles. This method is particularly effective for those whose earnings are steady or only modestly rising. It transforms uncertainty into certainty: the amounts may not be exact, but they are defensible. For the disciplined but cautious, it is a shield.

The live-year method, by contrast, is forward-facing. It involves estimating your current year's income as it unfolds, adjusting contributions quarterly. For a business on a steep growth curve—or a volatile income pattern—it prevents massive shortfalls. A start-up founder, for instance, who quadruples turnover in a single year would find the last-year method dangerously insufficient. Instead, she might take a percentage of gross receipts—say, 20 to 25 per cent, depending on expected deductions—and move it immediately into a separate tax reserve account. Each quarter, she refines the figure based on real results, ensuring that her estimates track reality. It is more demanding, requiring vigilance and flexibility, but it aligns payments with present capacity.

To see the difference, imagine two examples. A UK consultant earning £80,000 last year and expecting roughly the same this year can simply set aside one quarter of last year's liability (£16,000 ÷ 4 = £4,000 per quarter). His cash flow is stable, his risk of penalty nil. Meanwhile, an Indian software developer whose income leaps from ₹10 lakh last year to ₹25 lakh this year cannot rely on the past. She might set aside 30 per cent of each invoice into a tax account as payments arrive, ensuring liquidity when quarterly instalments fall due. For her, the live-year method is not optional—it is survival.

Underlying both methods is the principle of treating taxes not as an afterthought but as a *first claim* on income. Just as collected VAT or sales tax is never truly yours, so too is income tax on profits an obligation that accrues invisibly. By carving out estimates early, you avoid the illusion of excess. This is why percentage-based rules—say, 20 per cent of gross receipts or 30 per cent of net profits—remain enduringly popular among self-employed professionals. They are not precise, but they are conservative, and conservatism is a shield when future liabilities are at stake.

Yet there is also nuance. Gross-based set-asides (a flat slice of every payment received) are psychologically easier: every client payment is partly "business" and partly "tax." Net-based set-asides (a slice of profit after expenses) are theoretically tighter but require real-time tracking of costs. One favours simplicity, the other accuracy. Both are valid; the choice depends on temperament. Those prone to overspending benefit from the rigidity of gross-based rules; those who track diligently may extract more efficiency from net-based ones.

What often surprises new business owners is how the choice of method shapes behaviour. Someone who religiously moves 25 per cent of every client payment into a separate account begins to see those reserves grow—visible, tangible reassurance. The act itself disciplines spending. By contrast, waiting to calculate on net income may foster a sense of freedom, but it risks leaving too little when expenses have crept higher than expected. Here, accounting method becomes not merely a technical choice but a behavioural nudge, steering how one perceives and manages money.

This raises a broader reflection: in finance, systems are as much about psychology as arithmetic. The "sanity" of an estimate lies not in its mathematical perfection but in its capacity to preserve peace of mind and liquidity. The best method is not the most exact, but the one that prevents panic, supports growth, and builds resilience. Tax estimation, then, is less about predicting the future and more about insulating yourself from it.

And yet, even with methods in place, questions remain. What happens in years of sudden downturn? How do you reconcile quarterly obligations with uneven monthly income? Can automation truly remove the friction, or does it risk dulling the awareness that sustains discipline? These tensions linger, suggesting that the art of sane estimation is never fully resolved. It is a balancing act, renewed each year, between the security of the past and the uncertainty of the future.

US/UK/Canada/India quick notes

For something as ancient as taxation, the architecture of deadlines and labels is curiously local. One person speaks of "quarterly instalments," another of "advance tax," another of "self-assessment." Yet beneath the linguistic clutter lies the same underlying principle: governments want their share as you earn, not long after the fact. The words may shift, the portals may differ, but the obligation is structurally alike—predictable in its intent, opaque only in its costume.

The United States is perhaps the most explicit about this rhythm. Here, "estimated tax payments" fall due four times a year—mid-April, mid-June, mid-September, and mid-January—through the Internal Revenue Service (IRS). The paradox is that the "January" payment technically belongs to the prior year, a reminder that tax calendars often bleed across the neat lines of our lived ones. The IRS's Electronic Federal Tax Payment System (EFTPS) or its more streamlined Direct Pay portal are the usual channels. For those steeped in payroll deductions, the system seems alien; for the self-employed, it is a relentless drumbeat. Pay-as-you-go is not simply a principle but a legal requirement, underpinned by penalties that punish hesitation.

Across the Atlantic, the United Kingdom uses different language but a similar logic. Here, "Payments on Account" are the mechanism—two instalments, each half of the prior year's bill, due at the end of January and July, with a balancing payment the following January if the year just ended was stronger. The HMRC online account becomes the hub, accessible with a government gateway login. The rhythm is less frenetic than the American four-step, but the sting is often sharper: January demands both the final settlement for the past year *and* the first advance payment for the current one. Many an unwary freelancer has found themselves short, realising too late that one cheque must serve two purposes.

Canada, pragmatic as ever, adds its own twist. Instalment payments are required for individuals whose net tax owing exceeds a modest threshold (currently around CAD 3,000 outside Quebec, CAD 1,800 within). Payments are quarterly—March, June, September, and December—through the Canada Revenue Agency's "My Payment" system or online banking. Here the threshold matters: many new businesses discover they are exempt from instalments in their first profitable year, only to be caught the next when their balance tips them over. Canada builds in both a grace period and a trigger, a recognition that not every earner is equally able to anticipate.

India's language is distinctive: *advance tax*. Yet the structure again is familiar. Instalments are due four times a year—15 June, 15 September, 15 December, and 15 March—via the Income Tax Department's online portal. Each instalment has a target percentage of the year's estimated liability (15 per cent, 45 per cent, 75 per cent, and finally 100 per cent). The Indian system, more granular in its escalating demands, illustrates a philosophy of constant reconciliation: each quarter is a checkpoint, not just a contribution. For businesses in fast-changing markets, this cadence can feel both exhausting and clarifying—it forces visibility.

What ties these systems together is not the surface mechanics but the deeper expectation: that citizens carry the burden of cash flow planning, not the state. Employers smooth the process for salaried staff through withholding; the self-employed and the entrepreneurial must recreate that machinery on their own. The naming conventions—estimated tax, payments on account, instalments, advance tax—are less about difference than about history. Each system reveals a culture's approach to compliance. The American insistence on quarterly payments reflects a suspicion of arrears. Britain's half-yearly rhythm mirrors an older accountancy cycle. Canada's threshold-based design shows a tolerance for smaller players. India's escalating instalments embody the state's demand for constant engagement.

And yet, the problem for the individual remains the same: to map one's own business cycle onto the state's calendar without slipping into crisis. The portals, deadlines, and terms are the scaffolding; what matters is the habit they enforce. To set money aside each month, to tie one's liquidity to these immovable dates, is less an act of compliance than of self-preservation.

Still, a question lingers, unresolved: if the systems are designed to align the citizen with the state's cash flow needs, do they also serve the citizen's stability—or merely the government's convenience? The answer may depend not on the dates themselves, but on how we integrate them into the fabric of our financial lives.

Automating the habit: Estimates are baked into the weekly ritual via earmarked funds and reminders, closing the loop between planning and action

The story of tax stress often begins with a calendar. A letter arrives, a reminder pings, a deadline is suddenly too close. Many entrepreneurs recall the shock of their first significant bill, payable not in theory but in cash they had already spent. The paradox is simple: earning money is exhilarating; setting it aside for the state feels like loss. Yet the difference between the confident and the anxious lies not in earnings but in systems. Those who automate thrive; those who improvise stumble.

The most disciplined among us know this truth: willpower is unreliable, memory is fragile, but structure endures. Athletes lace their shoes at the same hour every morning, not because they love waking at dawn but because routine spares them choice. The same principle applies to estimated taxes. To strip away the drama of quarterly payments, the habit must be shrunk down to a weekly ritual, folded into the rhythm of ordinary business. This is not about heroics in April or September; it is about an almost invisible gesture, repeated fifty-two times a year, that makes the extraordinary disappear into the ordinary.

At its simplest, automation begins with earmarking. A second bank account, dedicated solely to tax reserves, acts as a firewall between temptation and obligation. Each week—or each payment cycle—funds are siphoned off, not manually but by standing instruction. Whether it is 20 per cent of gross receipts, 30 per cent of net profit, or another figure suited to one's jurisdiction and growth, the key is not precision but predictability. The transfer becomes as unremarkable as rent or utilities, a cost of doing business rather than a discretionary afterthought. The entrepreneur who sees their "real" balance already net of tax never falls prey to illusions of surplus.

Technology makes this discipline lighter still. Modern accounting software, from QuickBooks to Xero, now offers automatic allocations, where each incoming payment is instantly split between operational funds, savings, and tax reserves. Digital banks provide "spaces" or "pots" that act like digital envelopes, invisibly partitioning cash. Mobile reminders, integrated into calendars or task apps, reinforce the ritual: every Friday at 4 p.m., review receipts, check the earmarked transfer, confirm the trail. Done consistently, it is no longer a burden but muscle memory.

The human mind, however, resists such structure until it has been tested. Here lies the deeper tension: we tend to trust ourselves more than systems, until experience proves the opposite. Consider the freelancer who, flush with a sudden £8,000 project, vows to "set aside something later." Weeks pass, the funds dwindle across rent, equipment, and an impulsive holiday, and by January the reserve is gone. Contrast this with the entrepreneur who has a standing order to sweep 25 per cent into a tax account the moment payment clears. The difference is not intelligence, nor moral fibre, but automation. One has externalised discipline; the other relies on memory.

The beauty of the weekly ritual lies not only in cash preservation but in emotional clarity. A quarterly payment can feel punitive—three months of work evaporating in a single transfer. A weekly allocation feels modest, proportionate, almost forgettable. The pain is distributed, the shock dissolved. Behavioural economists would recognise this as a framing effect: the same outcome, reframed into smaller, gentler increments, changes perception entirely. What felt like an imposition now feels like stewardship.

There is, too, a philosophical dimension. Taxes are often framed as interruptions—alien obligations that collide with the flow of business. But when automation makes them part of the weekly rhythm, they cease to be interruptions at all. They become part of the shape of the work, woven into its financial and moral fabric. Just as rent secures space and salaries secure people, reserves secure solvency. The entrepreneur is no longer a reluctant intermediary between client and state but a manager of flows, ensuring each party receives what is due.

Of course, perfection is unnecessary. No one needs to log every receipt or calculate every penny in real time. What matters is consistency. A modest error rate in weekly allocations, adjusted at year's end, is far less costly than a flawless calculation made once and then forgotten. Consistency without drama builds resilience; drama without consistency breeds collapse.

Cultural context reveals variations. In the United States, where four estimated payments punctuate the year, automation ensures each instalment arrives without panic. In the United Kingdom, with its January double hit, weekly sweeps prevent the dreaded scramble. In Canada, where instalments kick in above certain thresholds, automation provides readiness for the year when profits finally exceed the bar. In India, where four escalating percentages must be met, weekly allocations align the individual with the state's quarterly checkpoints. The mechanics differ, but the principle does not: embed the habit, and the system bends to you rather than the other way around.

And yet, a provocative question remains. If automation makes tax reserves invisible, almost painless, does it also dull our awareness of the state's demands? Do we risk reducing civic contribution to another line item, stripped of context, stripped of deliberation? Or is this precisely the point—that by removing resistance, we liberate energy for the work itself, leaving philosophy to the margins? The answer, perhaps, lies not in choosing one view or the other, but in recognising that automation is not merely financial hygiene. It is a statement about how we live with obligations: not as crises to be managed, but as habits to be honoured.

Chapter 8
Records That Think for You

The fall of many otherwise promising ventures begins not with a bad idea, but with bad records. It is almost always an unseen collapse before it becomes a visible one. An entrepreneur, confident in their instincts and fuelled by early revenue, delays setting up a dedicated account, commingles personal and business funds, and assures themselves they will "sort it later." Later, of course, arrives at the most inconvenient moment: a tax inspection, an investor request, a liquidity crunch. The numbers refuse to add up, not because the business is failing, but because the records have.

This fragility is not new. In the nineteenth century, as industrial firms swelled beyond the scale of a family workshop, the most valuable innovation was not the loom or the steam engine, but double-entry bookkeeping systems robust enough to keep creditors, shareholders, and governments convinced. Accuracy was not a luxury; it was survival. Today, the same truth endures: resilience comes less from ambition and more from how clearly one can prove, quickly and without hesitation, what has been earned, spent, and set aside.

Modern founders, however, face a peculiar paradox. The tools available—cloud software, bank feeds, AI categorisation, mobile receipt capture—are more powerful and cheaper than anything prior generations could imagine. Yet many businesses remain paralysed by tool churn, tempted by novelty, overwhelmed by granularity, and misled into thinking that more complex systems automatically mean more control. In reality, the reverse is often true: complexity breeds fragility, while discipline and simplicity build records that "think" for the business rather than burden it.

The backbone of this discipline is separation. A dedicated business account, ring-fenced from personal spending, is not only a practical safeguard but a symbolic act. It declares to the world—and to oneself—that the enterprise is real. It slashes categorisation time, transforms reconciliation from detective work into confirmation, and builds audit resilience by ending the blurred edges of co-mingling. The clarity purchased by a single account often outweighs the cleverness of any software layered on top.

From there, structure amplifies clarity. A three-bucket ledger—Revenue, Direct Costs, and Overheads—creates a grammar simple enough to survive across borders and industries. By resisting the temptation to fracture expenses into endless categories, founders prevent chaos at the review stage. Decision-ready reports emerge faster, anomalies reveal themselves more starkly, and trends are easier to act upon. In practice, this is the difference between spending an evening arguing over whether a subscription should be classed as "Software" or "Professional Services" and spending it identifying which costs can actually be trimmed.

The tools themselves, when chosen sparingly, should be allies rather than distractions. A minimal, reliable stack—bank feeds for flow, receipt capture for proof, and either a spreadsheet or entry-level accounting software for synthesis—has more staying power than a carousel of apps. Explicit trade-offs, declared at the outset, inoculate against tool churn: "This may not categorise every coffee purchase automatically, but it will be here in five years, and I will know how to use it." The most elegant stack is not the one that dazzles in a demo but the one that still functions in a crisis.

The final piece is cadence. A monthly close, performed in thirty minutes with a four-step script, transforms record-keeping from a dreaded task into a repeatable habit. Reconcile the bank. Review anomalies. Update set-asides. Export a snapshot. Done with discipline, this routine builds a muscle memory as durable as brushing teeth. What emerges is not only order but foresight: anomalies are caught before they metastasise, tax reserves are always current, and decisions are made on reality rather than recollection.

This chapter unfolds from these principles. It shows how records can become more than compliance artefacts—they can become decision engines. By setting the foundation with separation, reinforcing it with simple structure, resisting tool fetishism, and embedding cadence, entrepreneurs create records that do the thinking for them. The prize is more than audit readiness or reduced stress; it is the freedom to run a business without fear that the numbers will betray them. The challenge, however, remains timeless: to resist the allure of improvisation and complexity, and to commit instead to a discipline that feels almost mundane. For it is often the mundane rituals, invisible to the outside world, that guard the extraordinary from collapse.

Bank separation and the single source of truth: A dedicated business account is the backbone of clarity. It slashes categorisation time and lifts audit resilience by ending co-mingling.

The downfall of many small businesses begins not with strategy or sales, but with something far less dramatic: the blurring of personal and business finances. A founder swipes the same debit card for groceries and for supplier invoices. A freelancer pays rent from the same account that collects client fees. For months, perhaps years, nothing seems amiss—until an audit arrives, a funding opportunity demands proof of income, or a tax deadline looms. Suddenly, the absence of separation is not just inconvenient, but existential. The records cannot speak with a single voice.

History offers a telling lesson. When partnerships in Renaissance Italy formalised their operations, one of the first steps was the establishment of distinct ledgers—books that clearly divided a merchant's private dealings from the affairs of the firm. This separation was not merely a matter of tidiness. It was the foundation upon which accountability and trust could stand. Investors, partners, and tax collectors all required the same thing: confidence that the numbers represented the business and nothing else. What was true in Florence in 1494 remains true in London, Toronto, Delhi, or New York today.

A dedicated business bank account is more than administrative hygiene—it is a declaration of identity. It says: this is the business, distinct from the person who runs it. It creates a *single source of truth*, the backbone from which all reports, reconciliations, and filings are drawn. With one clean feed, the work of categorisation is slashed. Transactions fall naturally into business categories without the detective work of sorting through restaurant bills or cash withdrawals that might—or might not—be relevant.

The clarity compounds. With separate accounts, audits are transformed from adversarial interrogations into straightforward verifications. Regulators and tax authorities are less likely to question what they can easily trace. Lenders and investors are reassured by transparent numbers that match bank statements, not back-of-envelope reconstructions. For the business owner, stress decreases. No more end-of-year panic hunting for receipts to prove that a transaction was not personal. The story of the business writes itself, in real time, through the account.

Some argue that separation is unnecessary for the smallest of ventures—that a sole trader can get by with colour-coded spreadsheets or manual tagging of personal versus business spending. But these "efficiencies" quickly collapse under scrutiny. The time spent retroactively untangling mixed records almost always exceeds the effort of maintaining a distinct account from day one. More importantly, the lack of separation corrodes confidence. Without a crisp line, how persuasive can one be in defending deductions, negotiating terms, or seeking external capital? A small administrative shortcut today becomes a strategic liability tomorrow.

There is also a deeper psychological dimension. Keeping personal and business funds in the same pot blurs not just accounting categories, but mental boundaries. It fosters the illusion that revenue is instantly available for personal consumption, or conversely, that personal hardship justifies dipping into business reserves. Separation disciplines the entrepreneur as much as it disciplines the records. It turns the business into an entity that must stand on its own, living or dying by its own inflows and outflows, rather than being propped up—or drained—by its owner's whims.

Examples across jurisdictions reinforce this. In the United States, the Internal Revenue Service explicitly warns that co-mingling personal and business expenses undermines the credibility of claimed deductions. In the United Kingdom, HMRC guidance highlights the importance of separate records even for sole traders, noting that shared accounts invite unnecessary disputes. Canada and India echo the same theme: while the legal structures differ, the operational principle is universal. Separation is not optional if resilience is the goal.

What emerges, then, is a principle as much as a practice: one bank account, one truth. This simplicity resists the chaos of over-granular systems and the paralysis of tool churn. It provides the raw material for a streamlined ledger, for efficient reconciliations, and for credible filings. It is the keystone that allows the rest of the record-keeping architecture to stand.

The temptation, of course, is always to delay—especially when a business is young and cash is tight. But the question is not whether one can afford to open and maintain a separate account; it is whether one can afford the cost of not doing so. When the first serious investor asks for proof of revenue, or when the tax officer requests supporting documents, the founder who chose separation will have answers in minutes. The one who did not will scramble, reconstruct, and hope.

The difference between those two scenarios is not intelligence or ambition. It is discipline—the willingness to set boundaries that make truth visible. And so the unresolved challenge lingers: will the entrepreneur treat separation as a burden to be postponed, or as the quiet act of seriousness that secures the future?

The three-bucket ledger: Standardising categories into Revenue, Direct Costs, and Overheads prevents over-granular chaos and speeds review for decision-ready reports.

The paradox of modern bookkeeping is that more data often means less clarity. Walk into the back office of many small firms and you will find accounts bloated with categories: "stationery", "client meals", "subscription A", "subscription B", "miscellaneous (miscellaneous)". Each expense is carefully assigned, yet when the owner asks the simplest of questions—"Are we actually profitable?"—the system falls silent. The ledgers are full, but the story is obscured. Complexity has become the enemy of insight.

History offers a telling counterpoint. When double-entry bookkeeping spread across Renaissance Europe, its power lay not in excessive detail but in elegant structure. Merchants grouped transactions in ways that highlighted what truly mattered: inflows, outflows, and balances. Too much granularity would have drowned them in paper. Too little would have left them blind. The balance between precision and readability was itself a technology of trust. That principle has not aged.

At its heart, the three-bucket ledger restores this lost simplicity. Every transaction, no matter how messy in the moment, finds its home in one of three places: *Revenue*, *Direct Costs*, or *Overheads*. It is a mental model as much as an accounting rule, stripping away noise to reveal the essential dynamics of a business. A designer's invoice, a manufacturer's raw materials, a consultant's advertising spend—they all sort themselves naturally once the buckets are defined.

Revenue is the fuel. It represents the inflows from sales, services, or licensing—whatever the business does to earn its keep. Clarity here matters because revenue tells the world how effectively the enterprise creates value. When recorded in isolation, revenue also disciplines the imagination: a founder can no longer inflate their sense of success by confusing borrowed funds or capital injections with earned money. It is a clean, unambiguous number, resistant to self-deception.

Direct Costs are the inputs consumed in producing that revenue. The more tightly these are defined, the sharper the business's margin appears. For a café, direct costs include coffee beans and milk; for a software firm, server fees and outsourced development. Grouping them together transforms a list of petty expenses into a living measure of efficiency. It shows how much is being spent to generate each unit of income. In turbulent markets, this visibility is survival.

Overheads, by contrast, are the costs of being in business rather than of producing the specific product or service. They are the office rent, the insurance premiums, the professional fees—the background hum of activity without which the firm cannot operate. When thrown into the same pool as direct costs, overheads distort the true profitability of core activities. But when separated, they offer clarity:

one can distinguish between operational discipline and structural drag.

This tripartite system does more than neaten the books. It accelerates decision-making. Instead of wading through fifty categories to find patterns, an owner sees at a glance: revenue is steady, direct costs are creeping up, overheads are manageable. The architecture of the ledger itself encourages sharper questions: Are we charging enough? Are suppliers squeezing our margins? Are fixed costs proportionate to scale? The ledger becomes a decision tool, not just a compliance archive.

There is a psychological payoff, too. When categories proliferate, review sessions devolve into unproductive debates about classification: should software subscriptions go under IT or marketing? Does the office plant belong to supplies or décor? These debates consume energy without creating insight. The three-bucket system cuts through this by focusing on substance over semantics. The discussion shifts from "where to file" to "what does this number mean for our survival and growth?"

Critics sometimes argue that this approach oversimplifies—that by reducing accounts to three categories, businesses risk ignoring important nuances. But nuance is not the same as noise. Detailed subcategories can still exist within each bucket for internal tracking; what changes is the top-level structure. The ledger can always zoom in, but the essential story is told at the right altitude. And in practice, most small and mid-sized firms benefit far more from clarity at the strategic level than from exhaustive granularity at the operational level.

The model also travels well across borders and industries. While tax codes vary wildly—what qualifies as deductible in India may not in Canada, and UK treatment of VAT differs sharply from US sales tax—the principles of revenue, direct costs, and overheads are universal. This portability is powerful. It allows an entrepreneur in Mumbai to converse meaningfully with an investor in Toronto or a partner in London, without getting lost in translation. Numbers arranged into these three categories speak a common financial language.

Moreover, the three-bucket ledger resists one of the greatest dangers of modern entrepreneurship: tool churn. Many businesses, seduced by the promise of apps and dashboards, find themselves constantly migrating between platforms. Each migration produces new categories, new reporting templates, new frustrations. The buckets act as a stable backbone. Whether one is using a spreadsheet, entry-level accounting software, or advanced ERP, the three-bucket framework endures. It is a mental model that survives technological fashion.

The deeper insight is this: structure shapes perception. A cluttered ledger encourages scattered thinking, while a streamlined one fosters strategic discipline. When business owners sit down each month to review their finances, the structure of their accounts quietly frames the questions they ask and the answers they see. Choosing a three-bucket ledger is not just an administrative decision. It is a design choice about how reality will be perceived.

And so the lingering question remains: will one allow the ledger to dictate chaos through unchecked categories, or will one impose a structure that makes the truth immediately visible? In the end, the decision is not about bookkeeping at all. It is about whether the business is willing to see itself clearly—and act accordingly.

Lightweight tooling stack: A minimal, reliable stack—bank feeds, receipt capture, spreadsheet or entry-level software—beats novelty. Explicit trade-offs resist tool churn.

The business press loves a shiny tool. Every quarter, some new platform promises to "revolutionise" bookkeeping or "disrupt" financial management. Founders are told that without real-time dashboards, AI categorisation, or blockchain-enabled reconciliation, they are stuck in the dark ages. Yet talk privately with owners who have weathered years of growth, downturn, and recovery, and a different picture emerges. Their systems are often surprisingly modest: a dedicated bank account, a simple receipt-capture app, and a spreadsheet or entry-level software package. No fanfare, no churn. Just a toolkit that works.

The paradox is that novelty creates fragility. A business constantly chasing the latest tool spends more time migrating data, retraining staff, and fixing integration glitches than actually using its numbers to make decisions. This fragility compounds at the worst possible moment—during a tax filing, a funding round, or an audit—when stability matters most. In contrast, a deliberately minimalist stack provides resilience. It may lack glamour, but it functions reliably, month after month, year after year.

The first anchor is the *bank feed.* In principle, every financial transaction passes through the bank; it is the single source of truth. Automated feeds pull this information into a ledger or spreadsheet, eliminating human error in data entry. A clean feed slashes reconciliation time and grounds every report in verifiable fact. Without it, even the most sophisticated system risks floating free from reality, relying on assumptions rather than evidence.

The second anchor is *receipt capture.* Tax authorities across jurisdictions demand substantiation: a bank statement alone will rarely suffice. Lightweight capture tools—scanning apps, email-forward systems, or cloud folders—create a living archive of proof. The technology itself need not be complex; what matters is consistency. A photo of a restaurant bill, annotated with "client lunch, project X", may do more to defend a deduction than an elaborate expense-management suite. The discipline is what counts, and the tool's role is simply to make it effortless.

The third anchor is a *simple ledger*, whether a structured spreadsheet or a low-cost software package. The purpose here is not to impress with design but to enable swift categorisation, monthly reconciliation, and reporting that supports decisions. Entry-level packages may integrate bank feeds and receipt capture directly, while a spreadsheet demands more manual discipline. Either can succeed if the user is clear about what trade-offs they are accepting.

That word—*trade-offs*—is critical. The lightweight stack thrives not because it is universally superior, but because it forces explicit choices. A spreadsheet offers total control but little automation. Software automates but imposes its own taxonomy. The mature business owner resists the lure of "best of both worlds" marketing and instead selects the least painful compromise for their scale, staff capacity, and appetite for precision. Tool churn usually arises from a refusal to confront these trade-offs honestly.

There is also a cultural element. Teams accustomed to novelty often confuse activity with progress. They chase the dopamine hit of a new app rollout, while financial clarity—the true goal—slips further away. The quiet power of the lightweight stack is that it reduces novelty to the background. It allows owners and staff to focus on what the numbers actually *mean*. It embeds finance as a practice, not a distraction.

To illustrate, consider two firms. One uses a dozen integrated platforms: invoicing software, project-management billing, payroll systems, multi-currency expense trackers, each with its own subscription and support team. When a regulator requests a simple revenue reconciliation, the firm spends days exporting and stitching data together. The other firm uses a single ledger, fed by bank transactions and annotated with scanned receipts. When asked the same question, they produce a clean report in minutes. Which is truly "modern"?

None of this is to dismiss innovation. Larger organisations with complex structures may indeed require specialised systems. But for the vast majority of small and mid-sized businesses, the lightweight stack is not a compromise but a design principle: start with the minimum, ensure it works, and only add complexity if the case is undeniable. The default posture is scepticism towards novelty.

Philosophically, this approach echoes an older wisdom. The economist Herbert Simon observed that in decision-making, *satisficing*—settling for a solution that is "good enough"—often outperforms the quest for optimisation. The lightweight tooling stack embodies this. It is not perfect, but it is sufficient, reliable, and resistant to distraction. In the volatile landscape of entrepreneurship, "good enough and stable" usually beats "perfect and brittle".

And yet, the temptation never disappears. New tools will keep arriving, each with slicker interfaces and more seductive promises. The real question for any business is not *which tool to adopt*, but *how much instability it is willing to tolerate for the sake of novelty.* Will it commit to a stable, minimal architecture that allows the business itself to think clearly—or will it let its ledger become a laboratory for other people's experiments?

Monthly close in 30 minutes: A four-step script reconciles bank, reviews anomalies, updates set-aside, and exports a snapshot, building muscle memory for tax-smart operations.

The companies most admired for financial discipline are rarely those with the most elaborate systems. Instead, they are the ones that turn discipline into ritual. A simple routine, repeated without fail, outperforms the grand gesture executed inconsistently. Consider the restaurateur who, at the end of each week, wipes down every surface, checks the stock, and closes the till. None of these actions take long, but together they preserve order, readiness, and trust. The monthly financial close works the same way: a short ritual that prevents small discrepancies from snowballing into existential headaches.

The paradox is that many business owners see closing the books as a monumental task—one that demands a weekend lost to spreadsheets, chasing receipts, or deciphering bank statements. The reality is quite the opposite. When broken into a repeatable script, the monthly close can be completed in thirty minutes, sometimes less. The efficiency is not the result of cutting corners but of focusing only on what matters: reconciling, reviewing, adjusting, and capturing. By turning this into a habit, the business not only saves time but also builds a tax-smart reflex that pays dividends in resilience and confidence.

At the core of this ritual is the *reconciliation of the bank account.* If the bank is the single source of truth, then matching the ledger to it is non-negotiable. Every transaction must be accounted for, whether automatically pulled by feeds or entered manually. The act itself is deceptively simple: tick off what matches, investigate what doesn't. Yet its impact is profound. Reconciliation ensures that the financial record is not an abstraction but a mirror of reality. Without it, every report, every decision, rests on sand.

The second step is the *review of anomalies*. This is where the human eye adds value. Software can flag mismatches, but it cannot grasp context. An unexpected supplier charge, a double billing, or a subscription that has quietly crept up in cost—these are the kinds of anomalies that erode margins silently if left unchecked. By scanning for irregularities once a month, the owner prevents minor leaks from becoming major losses. Just as a ship's captain inspects the hull for cracks, the business owner inspects the books for fractures.

The third step is to *update set-asides*. Here lies the tax-smart element. Instead of waiting until year-end and facing a painful scramble, the monthly close reinforces a discipline: move a percentage of income into earmarked accounts for taxes, reserves, or strategic investments. This is not merely about mechanics but about psychology. By ring-fencing funds regularly, the business normalises prudence. The money ceases to feel like "available cash" and begins to serve its true purpose. In this way, the monthly close becomes not just about record-keeping but about future-proofing.

The final step is to *export a snapshot*. Numbers only serve if they can be seen. A simple report—balance, cash on hand, outstanding liabilities, current set-asides—captures the state of play. For the solo operator, this may live in a spreadsheet; for a growing team, it may form part of a dashboard or monthly briefing. The point is not sophistication but visibility. Without a snapshot, discipline stays locked inside a process. With it, discipline becomes insight, shared and actionable.

Taken together, these four steps form a script that is powerful precisely because it is ordinary. It demands no specialist training, no advanced tools, no heroic effort. But repetition builds something extraordinary: *muscle memory*. Just as an athlete no longer thinks consciously about foot placement or breathing rhythm, the owner who performs this monthly close begins to internalise financial control. It becomes instinctive, a natural extension of running the business.

And yet, one might ask: if it is so simple, why do so few businesses practice it? The answer is cultural. Finance has been mythologised as a domain of experts, burdened with jargon and mystique. The monthly close demystifies it. It takes control out of the accountant's quarterly reports and places it back in the hands of the owner, without supplanting the accountant's role. This rebalancing is both empowering and disquieting. Empowering because clarity is immediate; disquieting because it removes excuses.

Here lies the deeper philosophical point: the monthly close is not about bookkeeping but about stewardship. To close the books monthly is to acknowledge that money is not passive but active; it flows, it accumulates, it escapes, it needs direction. In neglecting this ritual, a business tacitly admits that it prefers ignorance over awareness. In embracing it, the business declares that it will face reality squarely, however uncomfortable.

The thirty-minute monthly close, then, is a threshold practice. Cross it regularly, and the business gains strength quietly, month by month. Neglect it, and fragility creeps in unnoticed until crisis strikes. The choice is deceptively small—a half-hour on the calendar—but the consequences echo far beyond. Will the business choose to build resilience through ritual, or will it leave its financial health to drift, uninspected, until the day the silence breaks?

Chapter 9
Working with an Accountant (and When Not To)

The word *accountant* evokes an odd duality. For some, it conjures a trusted adviser—the calm presence who transforms financial confusion into clarity. For others, it means dread: bills for work they don't understand, explanations that feel opaque, or the sinking suspicion that the professional relationship is more extractive than supportive. Yet this contradiction is less about accountants themselves and more about how business owners approach them. Too often, founders treat accountants as glorified bookkeepers or compliance clerks, buying hours instead of outcomes. And in doing so, they miss the real value that a skilled accountant can bring.

Consider the story of a small technology firm that, in its first years, outsourced everything financial to an accountant. Every receipt, every query, every tax calculation was placed into their hands. Fees ballooned, yet when a regulatory window closed, the business still faced penalties. Contrast this with a manufacturing start-up that treated its accountant not as a default processor but as a strategist. The founders did their own monthly reconciliations, maintained a clean package of records, and engaged their accountant primarily for planning: identifying tax shelters, timing capital purchases, and modelling cash-flow risk. Their fees were lower, their relationship stronger, and their outcomes far better. The difference lay not in the competence of the professionals, but in how intelligently the firms set the boundaries of the relationship.

The paradox is clear: accountants are most valuable when you need them least for routine. Their worth lies in interpretation, in pattern recognition, in spotting exposures you hadn't considered. A great accountant maps risk, not just records expenses; highlights opportunities, not just obligations. They work in the liminal spaces—the planning windows where decisions are reversible and leverage is greatest. Yet, because many business owners outsource too broadly, they burn resources on the low-value work that founders can handle themselves with modest effort.

What emerges, then, is a discipline of choice. Knowing when to rely on an accountant, and when not to, becomes a core business skill. This chapter explores four dimensions of that discipline. First, the real substance of what great accountants actually do, beyond the caricature of calculators and spreadsheets. Second, the art of the hand-off package: how a tidy, structured set of reconciliations, invoices, and clear questions can halve your fees and double the quality of advice. Third, the craft of interviewing and choosing: probing for responsiveness, jurisdictional expertise, and red flags that reveal more than glossy brochures ever could. And finally, the careful drawing of DIY boundaries: deciding which tasks you should always own and which ones are worth outsourcing, not only to save money but to avoid the false economy of abdication.

The stakes here are more than administrative. A business that over-delegates loses sight of its financial pulse; a business that under-delegates risks paralysis or costly errors. The right balance builds not only efficiency but resilience. It allows you to preserve control where it matters, while drawing on deep expertise where it counts.

The accountant, then, is not a fixture to be hired unquestioningly but a partner to be chosen deliberately. In the chapters ahead, we strip away illusions, highlight practices that work, and provide a framework for building relationships with accountants that are measured not in hours billed but in outcomes achieved. The question you will face is not simply *which accountant to hire* but *when to invite one in, and when to keep the work in your own hands*. That tension—between autonomy and reliance—is where the smartest businesses thrive.

What great accountants actually do: Real value is risk mapping, planning windows, and high-leverage corrections. Stop buying hours; start buying outcomes.

The founder of a small design studio once thought she was buying peace of mind by paying her accountant for every conceivable task: sorting invoices, reconciling bank feeds, even chasing receipts. The bills mounted. Yet when a subtle change in VAT thresholds passed unnoticed, she found herself staring at a penalty that erased years of "peace of mind" in a single letter from the tax authority. By contrast, a rival studio owner, who insisted on doing her own monthly reconciliations, brought her accountant into the conversation only twice a year—once for mid-year tax planning, once for year-end strategy. Her fees were lower, her compliance airtight, and her cash flow optimised. Both business owners had accountants of equal technical ability. The difference was that one was buying hours, while the other was buying outcomes.

This paradox sits at the heart of the modern accountant's value. Accountants are not, in truth, valuable for counting. Machines now do that cheaply, and software does it nearly flawlessly. What separates a mediocre accountant from a great one is not their ability to categorise expenses or produce ledgers, but their ability to map risk, spot planning windows, and apply high-leverage corrections at precisely the right time. Their true work is not about filling out the past but shaping the future.

Risk mapping is perhaps the least understood but most powerful function of a skilled accountant. Every business swims in a sea of potential exposures—tax audits, cash-flow squeezes, misclassified expenses, regulatory shifts. The founder's instinct is often to react to what is visible: a looming bill, a short-term funding need, a sudden growth spurt. The accountant, by contrast, is trained to see invisible fault lines. A good one can look at your revenue trajectory and spot that your structure is about to trigger a tax bracket shift. They can warn that your "innocent" staff perks are crossing into taxable benefit territory. They can highlight that your overseas client contracts, if structured wrongly, could drag you into a second jurisdiction's tax net. Risk mapping is not paranoia—it is foresight turned into protection.

Planning windows are the other half of the story. These are the moments when decisions can be made with disproportionate effect, when a small adjustment opens a large advantage. For example, deferring a single equipment purchase by three weeks might shift it into the next tax year, aligning expense recognition with a higher-profit period. Electing a change in corporate structure before revenues cross a certain threshold can transform the effective tax rate for years. Planning windows close quickly, and once they do, corrections are far more costly or even impossible. A great accountant's value lies in spotting these windows early and making sure the founder understands the trade-offs before time erases the opportunity.

Then there are high-leverage corrections—the interventions that turn near-disaster into recovery. A neglected payroll filing that could have spiralled into fines can be mitigated with the right voluntary disclosure. A messy trial balance can be realigned in a way that not only satisfies auditors but sharpens the clarity of management reporting. An accountant with strategic vision does not just mop up errors; they redesign the system so that the same error cannot recur. The leverage is in the correction's permanence—it creates a new baseline of resilience.

The tension is that most founders don't know how to measure this value. They look at accountants the way they look at plumbers: people you pay for time spent on visible tasks. But accounting is not plumbing; it is cartography. A plumber fixes leaks. An accountant draws maps—of cash, of obligations, of opportunities—and then hands you the compass. Hours spent on paperwork are a cost centre. Outcomes like avoided penalties, captured deductions, or optimised cash reserves are profit centres.

There is also a philosophical shift buried here. To treat your accountant as a technician is to narrow them into a compliance cage. To treat them as a strategist is to recognise that financial systems are living organisms, influenced by regulation, markets, and human error. A great accountant provides not simply answers, but orientation. They show you not just what the rules *are*, but how to play within them with grace and foresight.

This does not mean accountants are infallible. Some lean heavily into salesmanship, promising value but delivering standardised templates. Others cling to hourly billing models that reward inefficiency rather than insight. The discerning founder has to learn to test: to ask for scenario planning rather than historical reporting, to probe for jurisdiction-specific fluency rather than generic reassurance, to demand clarity in trade-offs rather than vague promises of "saving tax." An accountant who resists these conversations is signalling their limits.

The deeper point is this: the true function of a great accountant is to expand the founder's field of vision. They do not replace your judgement, but they sharpen it. They cannot eliminate risk, but they can show you which risks are worth taking and which will cripple you. They cannot guarantee outcomes, but they can map the landscape so that you are never surprised by its contours.

So the question for any business owner becomes unavoidable: are you buying hours, or outcomes? Are you paying someone to process what already happened, or to shape what happens next? The former is comfortable but low-yield. The latter requires engagement, preparation, and partnership—but the payoff is leverage across years. The uneasy truth is that many founders never make this shift. They remain trapped in the illusion that compliance equals safety, and that bills reflect value. Those who do make the shift discover that the accountant is not simply a record-keeper but a strategist, a cartographer of risk and opportunity.

And once you see them that way, a more unsettling question follows: if your accountant isn't mapping your risks, spotting your planning windows, or steering you toward high-leverage corrections—are they truly your accountant at all?

The hand-off package: A tidy packet—trial balance, reconciliations, key invoices, questions—cuts fees and errors, speeding filings and building rapport.

One of the great paradoxes of professional services is that the more effort a client puts in upfront, the less they end up paying. A founder who drops a shoebox of receipts on their accountant's desk is often shocked when the final bill is higher, not lower, than that of a peer who carefully assembled a packet of clean reconciliations and essential invoices. The difference is not only about efficiency; it is about respect. A disorganised hand-off signals indifference, leaving the accountant to guess, patch, and chase. A well-prepared one establishes trust, sets the tone for collaboration, and—most importantly—creates the conditions for better outcomes.

The hand-off package is not busywork. It is the bridge between the daily messiness of running a business and the ordered clarity of financial filings. At its core, it contains four pillars: a trial balance that shows the skeleton of the accounts; reconciliations that prove the numbers are tethered to reality; key invoices that capture the most consequential movements; and a short list of questions to flag ambiguities. Together, these items form a compact narrative of the year—a story that an accountant can read quickly, trust immediately, and build upon with confidence.

The trial balance is the backbone. It condenses the ledger into a single view, with debits and credits aligned. For the founder, producing one is not about mastering technical accounting—it is about discipline. It says, "I have reviewed my own records to a point of internal coherence." To an accountant, that statement is worth hours of time. Without it, they must reconstruct the balance themselves, often discovering inconsistencies late in the process when deadlines loom and corrections are more costly.

Reconciliations are the muscles. Bank accounts, credit cards, and payment platforms need to tie back to statements, month by month. This is not glamorous work, but it transforms loose data into defensible numbers. Without reconciliations, the accountant is forced to dig through anomalies, guessing whether a missing £500 is an overlooked expense or a mistyped deposit. With reconciliations, that same £500 is either explained or eliminated before the hand-off. The saving is not only in fees, but in accuracy. Errors caught at this stage prevent cascading misstatements in tax filings, loan applications, or future audits.

Key invoices are the beating heart. Not every invoice matters equally. A year of coffee receipts is noise; the three large equipment purchases that shift depreciation schedules are signal. By curating the most consequential documents—whether contracts, asset purchases, or unusual expenses—the founder spares the accountant from wading through trivia and directs attention to the items where interpretation matters. This is not cherry-picking; it is triage. It acknowledges that professional judgement is most valuable when applied to significant thresholds, not to stationery bills.

Finally, questions are the voice. No hand-off package is complete without a short list of open issues: "Is this software subscription capitalisable?" "Does this overseas client payment trigger withholding?" "Should this director loan be cleared before year-end?" These questions do two things. They prevent silent errors from being carried forward unnoticed. And they invite dialogue rather than assumption. Accountants who receive thoughtful questions respond not only with answers but with insights, often highlighting risks or opportunities the founder had not considered.

The benefits compound. A tidy packet reduces fees because it cuts duplication of effort. It reduces errors because the accountant starts with reconciled, structured data. It speeds filings because clarity accelerates review. And it builds rapport, because professionals respect clients who respect their time. More subtly, it reframes the relationship itself. The founder stops being a passive consumer of compliance and becomes an active partner in financial stewardship.

There is a deeper lesson here about ownership. Handing off a mess does not merely cost money; it abdicates control. If you cannot explain your own numbers even at a basic level, you cannot claim to be steering your business with intention. Preparing a clean hand-off is not simply about tidiness; it is about accountability. It forces the founder to see their enterprise not only as a swirl of projects and payments but as a structured system whose health must be measured, tested, and defended.

Yet many resist. They argue that accountants are paid to "sort it out," or that their time is better spent on sales, product, or strategy. There is truth in that—time is scarce. But this misses the strategic leverage of the hand-off. An hour spent assembling reconciliations saves three hours of accountant time, reduces the risk of misstatement, and builds goodwill that pays off in proactive advice down the line. The founder who invests that hour is not just saving money; they are purchasing clarity.

The irony is that the best accountants themselves quietly prefer clients who bring order. Not because it makes their lives easier, but because it allows them to do the higher-order work they are trained for: tax planning, risk assessment, structural advice. When bogged down by missing receipts and mislabelled payments, their expertise is wasted. When handed a tidy package, they can elevate the conversation from *what happened* to *what's possible.*

So the hand-off package is more than an administrative task—it is a statement of philosophy. It says: I take my numbers seriously. I respect my counterpart's time. I want our collaboration to focus not on patching the past, but on planning the future. The packet becomes not merely a folder of documents, but a gesture of partnership.

The question, then, is not whether you can afford the time to prepare it. The real question is whether you can afford the fog that comes without it. When the next filing season arrives, will you hand your accountant a clear story ready to be sharpened—or a mystery they must solve at your expense?

How to interview and decide: A discovery script tests scenarios, responsiveness, and jurisdiction specifics. Red flags and good signals empower confident choices.

Hiring an accountant can feel deceptively simple. On the surface, you are buying a service, no different from finding a lawyer or a doctor. Yet ask founders who have been burned by mismatched advisers, and you hear the same refrain: "I assumed competence. I only discovered fit after it was too late." The paradox is stark—most people devote more rigour to test-driving a car than to interviewing the person who will steer their financial compliance and planning.

Consider the case of a start-up founder in London who hired the cheapest accountant she could find, dazzled by assurances of low fees and fast filings. Six months later, when the company received a tax authority query about missed VAT obligations, the accountant went silent. Not malicious, simply overwhelmed and inattentive. The founder learned the hard way: you do not hire an accountant for their promises when things are smooth; you hire them for their response when the storm hits. An interview, done properly, surfaces those differences before the ink is dry.

At its best, interviewing an accountant is not a polite chat about services. It is a discovery process—structured, intentional, designed to test judgement under pressure. A well-crafted script does more than check qualifications; it explores responsiveness, anticipates edge cases, and probes jurisdictional fluency. The aim is to shift the balance of power. Instead of passively accepting the accountant's sales pitch, the founder becomes the examiner, drawing out signals—good and bad—that reveal the professional's true value.

The first axis of exploration is responsiveness. Imagine presenting a scenario: "If the tax authority sends a query letter with a two-week deadline, how do you respond?" A strong accountant will outline a process: immediate acknowledgement, document review, draft response, and client confirmation before submission. A weak one will wave it off with vague assurances. In that difference lies the measure of whether you are buying reliability or risk. Responsiveness is not about speed for its own sake; it is about the predictability of care.

The second axis is scenario-based judgement. It is easy for an accountant to claim experience; it is harder for them to walk through a hypothetical. "If my business shifts from freelancing to employing staff across borders, what are the first three compliance issues you flag?" Their answer reveals both depth and structure: do they think payroll and withholding? Do they mention permanent establishment rules? Do they highlight VAT thresholds? A crisp, organised response signals not only knowledge but the ability to prioritise in real time—an indispensable trait when your business evolves.

Jurisdictional fluency is the third test. In an increasingly global economy, even small firms touch multiple tax systems. Here, precision matters. A Canadian accountant who understands CRA rules but blurs the lines with U.S. obligations is a liability, not an adviser. A British accountant who knows HMRC's quirks about home office deductions but stumbles on cross-border VAT thresholds is under-equipped. The interview is the moment to ask directly: "What do you not handle?" A confident professional will name their limits and, ideally, point you to trusted partners. A hesitant one will over-promise, planting the seeds of future disappointment.

Yet, for all the structure, interviews also hinge on subtler cues—the good signals and red flags that do not appear in a résumé. A good signal: the accountant asks you questions that show genuine curiosity about your business model, not just your balance sheet. They want to understand how you make money, not just how you record it. A red flag: they speak in jargon without pausing to explain. If they cannot communicate clearly in a meeting, they will not communicate clearly under audit stress.

Another good signal: they outline trade-offs. For example, they might say, "We can maximise your deductions here, but it raises audit risk. Alternatively, we can take a more conservative route with less financial upside but higher defensibility." That candour is gold. The absence of it—the glossy promise of "maximum refund, no risk"—should chill the room. Tax is not a game of winning everything; it is a discipline of calibrated choices.

Philosophically, interviewing an accountant is about aligning incentives. You are not buying hours; you are buying outcomes: fewer surprises, better foresight, stronger resilience. An accountant who bristles at being tested, or who frames your probing as mistrust, may not be ready for the kind of collaborative partnership modern founders require. Conversely, an accountant who embraces the script, who enjoys stress-testing scenarios, reveals themselves not just as a technician but as a thinker—a co-pilot in strategy, not a back-office clerk.

The irony is that most founders do not prepare for these interviews. They arrive with vague questions—"What do you charge?" "Do you have experience with small businesses?"—and leave with equally vague answers. The discovery script reframes the conversation. It demands specifics. It transforms the interview from a formality into a filter, where competence, responsiveness, and judgement either shine or falter under gentle pressure.

What emerges, then, is a shift in mindset. Choosing an accountant is not about avoiding mistakes at the margins—it is about shaping the foundation of trust on which years of financial decisions will rest. The right interview process is not adversarial; it is clarifying. It allows both sides to decide whether the partnership has legs.

And so the founder faces a question that lingers beyond the interview room: if your accountant cannot answer well when stakes are hypothetical, how will they perform when stakes are real?

DIY boundaries: Tasks ideal for founders vs those worth outsourcing are mapped to protect budgets without false economies

There is a curious paradox in business finance: the same founder who would never attempt their own root canal may happily wrestle with tax filings at midnight. The motive is understandable—control, cost-saving, and the sense of being "hands-on." Yet just as dentistry without training courts disaster, there are financial tasks where founder involvement becomes an expensive form of false economy. The art lies not in doing everything yourself, nor in outsourcing blindly, but in drawing boundaries—knowing which duties sharpen a founder's insight and which only drain attention.

A story from Silicon Valley captures this tension. A first-time entrepreneur, proud of her frugality, managed her own payroll across three states. It worked until an employee moved abroad, triggering foreign withholding requirements she had never heard of. The penalties and retroactive filings wiped out the very savings she thought she had secured. Her lesson was not that founders should avoid financial tasks entirely, but that discernment—choosing what to own and what to hand off—is more valuable than raw persistence.

The distinction begins with tasks that build direct understanding. Founders benefit from preparing and reviewing their own cash flow forecasts. They gain a visceral sense of how money moves in and out, which no accountant can substitute. Recording expenses in broad categories can also be worthwhile in the early stages: it sharpens awareness of cost structures and forces decisions about priorities. These activities cultivate financial literacy—the foundation for intelligent delegation later on. Doing them yourself is not wasted labour; it is apprenticeship in your own enterprise.

Contrast that with the arcane technicalities of compliance. Tax return preparation, payroll filings, multi-jurisdiction VAT submissions—these are the domains where mistakes have exponential costs. Here, DIY ceases to be empowerment and becomes recklessness. The rules shift constantly; deadlines are unforgiving; penalties are indifferent to good intentions. Outsourcing these functions to professionals is not indulgence but prudence. It shields the founder's time while ensuring that compliance rests on expertise, not improvisation.

The boundary, then, is not binary but strategic. The founder should own tasks that strengthen decision-making and situational awareness, while outsourcing those where error margins are slim and consequences harsh. Consider reconciliations. A founder might review bank statements monthly to understand anomalies, but expect the accountant to prepare the trial balance. Or take invoicing: the founder should oversee terms and relationships, while a bookkeeper manages the mechanics of chasing late payments. This split maximises both control and efficiency.

A further dimension is rhythm. Some tasks reward daily or weekly founder attention: monitoring receivables, setting aside funds for tax, approving large expenses. Others, like quarterly VAT or annual statutory filings, emerge at intervals too long for a founder to maintain competence in without constant re-learning. Outsourcing these infrequent, technical processes liberates mental bandwidth for higher-value concerns. Time, after all, is the scarcest resource of a founder.

False economies often arise when founders misprice their own hours. Imagine spending ten hours struggling with payroll software to save £150 in fees. If your business time is worth £100 an hour in potential revenue, you have "saved" £150 while sacrificing £1,000 of opportunity. Worse, the task itself becomes a source of frustration rather than strategic insight. The allure of thrift blinds many to the hidden cost of misplaced DIY.

Yet outsourcing carries its own risks if done indiscriminately. A founder who delegates all financial visibility may wake to find that decisions are made on autopilot, detached from business reality. The relationship with money becomes mediated entirely through third parties, leaving the founder blind to brewing crises. Thus, even in delegation, oversight is non-negotiable. The founder's eye must remain on dashboards, summaries, and anomalies—even if someone else prepares the numbers.

Philosophically, this is a question of stewardship. Founders are custodians of their enterprise's financial integrity. To abdicate entirely is negligence; to hoard tasks out of fear or miserliness is folly. The wise course is balance: to master enough of the mechanics to interrogate advisers intelligently, while reserving professional tasks for professionals. It is less about ego—"I can do it all myself"—and more about humility: recognising where others' expertise serves the business better.

The boundary lines will not be identical for every founder. A former auditor turned entrepreneur may comfortably manage her own ledgers in the early years, while a visionary with no financial background may outsource bookkeeping from day one. What matters is not conformity to a single template, but conscious choice. DIY should be deliberate, not default. Outsourcing should be strategic, not reactive.

And so the founder confronts the question with no static answer: where, at this stage of the business, is your time best spent? The line between useful involvement and costly distraction shifts as companies grow. Today's empowering DIY task may become tomorrow's bottleneck. Recognising that shift in time is the real test of financial wisdom.

Chapter 10
Audits Without Drama

The word *audit* has an almost mythical power to unsettle. For many, it conjures the image of a government envelope dropping through the letterbox like a summons, or the vision of a stern official poring over receipts with surgical precision. Yet strip away the folklore and the fear, and an audit is less about sudden ambush than about patterns: anomalies in numbers, habits of sloppiness, and signals that catch the eye of an authority trained to notice what others overlook. The real surprise is not that audits happen, but that they often follow the same tell-tale markers—mismatched forms, unusual ratios, swings too wild to ignore, or neglected sales-tax records. What appears as a bolt from the blue is often the echo of earlier, preventable choices.

History offers reminders of this dynamic. The earliest tax inspectors in imperial China, Rome, and Britain relied not on omniscience but on inconsistencies: farmers who declared a yield too small compared to their neighbours, merchants whose customs duties veered from the expected, estates where estate levies were oddly light. The principle endures. Modern revenue agencies, armed with data analytics, use much the same lens—spotting the outliers, the deviations, the sloppy trails that hint at deeper issues. In other words, audits are rarely random; they are stories triggered by numbers that do not quite add up.

This chapter enters that terrain without flinching. It asks: what really happens when an audit begins, and how can preparation turn what is feared into what is manageable? The choreography of an audit, from the first letter through to closure, is rarely dramatic when understood. It is a series of predictable steps: requests for documents, clarifications, reconciliations, and, occasionally, negotiations. What counts is not rhetorical persuasion but evidence—files in order, receipts matched, explanations crisp. The aim is not to win an argument, but to demonstrate, beyond doubt, that the record speaks for itself.

Here lies a deeper insight: the most powerful audit defence is not reactive eloquence but proactive structure. An *evidence file*—a binder, physical or digital, maintained quietly throughout the year—becomes a shield. Within it sit reconciliations, key invoices, notes to explain decisions, and memos that capture context long forgotten. In a dispute over intent, this file speaks louder than memory, turning potential debates into closed questions. What looks like bureaucracy in the moment proves, later, to be resilience.

Yet even the best-prepared entrepreneur may face decisions under pressure: when to concede on a point, when to escalate to appeal, and how to weigh the costs of each path. These are not merely financial choices but philosophical ones—about the value of time, the preservation of relationships, and the precedent set for future dealings. To fight every issue to the bitter end may feel righteous but risks draining cash and focus. To concede everything may preserve peace but erodes principle. Navigating this spectrum demands a framework, not improvisation.

The promise of this chapter is simple: to strip away the drama without diminishing the seriousness. It will trace the triggers that invite audits, outline how the process actually unfolds, and reveal the practical systems that transform response into routine. Above all, it will arm you with the perspective that an audit is not an existential threat, but a test of discipline, clarity, and foresight. The reader who turns these pages will not be promised immunity from scrutiny—no one is—but will instead be equipped to face it with calm, precision, and the confidence that preparation always outruns panic.

The question that lingers is not whether audits can be avoided, but whether you will meet them as a scramble or as a rehearsal already mastered. That tension—between dread and discipline, fear and foresight—runs through what follows. And in exploring it, you may find that what once seemed like a confrontation becomes instead an affirmation of order.

What triggers attention: Red flags include mismatched forms, outlier ratios, wild swings, and sloppy sales-tax handling. Each links back to earlier preventative habits.

The summons of an audit rarely begins with human suspicion. It begins with a machine. A line of code scanning millions of returns, flagging a figure that does not conform to pattern, a ratio that makes no sense, a sudden swing that defies past behaviour. To the person filing, it may seem arbitrary. To the system reading, it is statistical certainty. The paradox is that the audit feels personal only because the trigger was impersonal: numbers that would not sit quietly alongside their neighbours.

Consider the case of a small consultancy whose turnover doubled in a year while its declared expenses hardly shifted. To the founder, this was a story of growth, restraint, and discipline. To the tax authority, it was a statistical outlier. Revenue without proportionate cost either suggested miraculous efficiency or a missing ledger of claims. The inevitable letter was not a judgment on character but a prompt to explain what the data could not reconcile.

These triggers matter because they expose the hidden language of compliance: the patterns that tax authorities expect and the deviations that rouse their curiosity. The forms you submit are not read in isolation but cross-checked against other filings, industry averages, and even external data sources. A mismatch between reported income on a tax return and the figure provided by a bank or client in an information slip is one of the most common sparks for further inquiry. The lesson is stark but liberating: consistency is not a luxury, it is survival.

Mismatched forms lie at the heart of many avoidable audits. A contractor who reports £85,000 in gross income while a client's slip shows £87,000 invites scrutiny, even if the discrepancy stems from timing or rounding. The modern system does not ask whether you intended deception; it asks only whether the numbers reconcile. Here, the preventative habit is almost embarrassingly simple: align figures meticulously before submission. An hour of reconciliation each quarter is worth more than days spent answering audit queries later.

Outlier ratios are another form of red flag. Tax authorities benchmark businesses against their peers. A café whose declared cost of goods sold is 10% of revenue where the industry norm is 30–40% will attract attention. Either the business has cracked a model that defies economics, or it has underreported costs or overstated income. Neither sits comfortably with the expectations of auditors. For the business owner, awareness of these norms allows for anticipation: unusual figures may be valid, but they demand documentation. When the narrative is clear and evidence ready, what looks like a deviation becomes a defensible distinction.

The same applies to **wild swings**. Year-to-year volatility is not inherently suspect—markets collapse, pandemics reshape demand, contracts dry up overnight. But large, unexplained movements without corresponding notes suggest a lack of transparency. A retailer whose revenue halves while costs remain flat cannot expect the silence of the tax office. To prevent misinterpretation, keep contemporaneous records: memos explaining extraordinary circumstances, correspondence about cancelled contracts, or board minutes on major business pivots. The paper trail ensures the swing reads as reality, not manipulation.

Perhaps the most overlooked trigger is **sloppy sales-tax handling**. Value-added tax (VAT) in the UK, GST in Canada and India, sales tax in parts of the US—all are transactional, visible, and unforgiving. A late payment here, a misapplied exemption there, and the system notices. Unlike corporate tax, which unfolds annually, sales tax is a drumbeat of monthly or quarterly compliance. Its errors are harder to hide because they surface in the flow of cash itself. And once attention lands here, it often spreads. If the short-term taxes are messy, auditors assume the annual filings may be worse.

Seen together, these triggers do not merely highlight potential errors. They form a mirror of discipline—or its absence. Mismatched forms point back to the habit of reconciliation. Outlier ratios reveal whether you know your industry context. Wild swings test your willingness to explain the exceptional. Sloppy sales-tax filings show whether you respect the rhythm of compliance. Each red flag is not just a number; it is a reflection of an underlying practice. The tax authority does not peer into your mind, but it infers habits from what the numbers suggest.

There is a philosophical tension here. On one hand, businesses want to be seen as dynamic, unique, even exceptional. On the other, tax systems thrive on conformity, predictability, and comparability. To the entrepreneur, innovation is a badge of honour. To the revenue officer, it is a deviation demanding evidence. This clash is not malicious; it is structural. Recognising it early prevents resentment. It also reframes the audit not as a moral trial but as a statistical consequence of standing out.

And yet, some triggers will always be beyond control. Growth that outpaces peers, crises that crater results, or legitimate structures that look unconventional will inevitably stand out. The task is not to eliminate risk but to translate it—to ensure the records already contain the answers. In this sense, audit-readiness is less about hiding anomalies than about narrating them before the question arises.

The unresolved tension is this: can you build systems so robust that the anomalies of life never escalate into suspicion? Or will there always be a gap between how businesses live and how authorities measure? That gap, narrow but persistent, is where the discipline of record-keeping must prove itself—not by erasing red flags, but by making them intelligible.

How audits actually unfold: From letter to closure, the choreography is explained so responses are precise and timely. Documentation beats persuasion.

The first sign rarely arrives with drama. There is no knock at the door, no stern inspector with a briefcase. It comes instead as a letter—ordinary in appearance, extraordinary in consequence. A thin envelope or a digital notice lands, its language polite but unmistakable: *your return has been selected for review.* At that moment, everything changes. The long months of filing, reconciling, and calculating are no longer abstract. They are about to be tested in a process as structured as a dance and as unforgiving as a court.

One might assume audits are battles of persuasion, of eloquence against bureaucracy. They are not. They are contests of records against records, timelines against timelines. The tax authority already believes in its algorithms; your task is not to charm them out of suspicion but to demonstrate, point by point, that your numbers hold up. This is why those who keep meticulous evidence often emerge unscathed, while those who improvise find themselves paying dearly not for fraud, but for disorganisation.

The choreography of an audit follows a sequence designed for efficiency, not intimidation. It begins with the **opening letter**, which specifies the scope: perhaps one year's VAT filings, or a focus on income reporting, or a particular deduction category. Contrary to myth, not every audit is a sweeping investigation of your entire financial life. Often, it is narrow, targeted, and can be closed swiftly—if the response is equally precise.

The first decision you face is strategic: respond directly or engage representation. Accountants familiar with audit practice often recommend becoming the *curator* rather than the *performer*. You collect the evidence, but they speak to the examiner. This separation matters because what feels like harmless context to a business owner may sound like unnecessary complication to an auditor. Precision of language matches precision of records.

Once the letter is received, the **document-gathering phase** begins. Here, the audit tests habits built months and years before. If you have reconciled bank statements, archived receipts, and annotated anomalies, producing the requested evidence is no more disruptive than pulling files from a drawer. If you have not, the audit becomes a scramble: reconstructing events, calling clients for copies, and defending memory against official records. The irony is cruel—those who worked hardest to grow their business but neglected their books often suffer the most, not for wrongdoing but for chaos.

The next stage is **submission and exchange**. You provide documents in the requested format, whether physical copies, digital uploads, or via a secure portal. The examiner reviews them, sometimes asking for clarifications or additional records. The process may feel slow, but it is deliberately methodical. Every figure must be traced, every inconsistency explained. It is here that the discipline of audit-readiness shows its worth: a clear memo attached to an unusual transaction can dissolve suspicion instantly, while a vague explanation can prolong the exchange for months.

Occasionally, the audit moves to an **in-person or virtual meeting**, though these are rarer than most fear. When they occur, the focus is narrow: walking through selected items, testing whether documentation supports the narrative. This is not a trial but a verification exercise. The auditor is not interested in your story of entrepreneurial grit or market conditions; they are interested in whether the invoice matches the entry, whether the tax form reconciles with the bank feed. Here, persuasion has no power—only documentation.

As the review progresses, two paths diverge. In the smooth case, the evidence aligns, the questions are answered, and the **closure letter** arrives. Relief is palpable, but the experience often changes behaviour permanently: businesses that endure an audit tend to maintain sharper records forever after. In the more difficult case, discrepancies remain. These can lead to adjustments—additional tax assessed, penalties applied, or, in rare cases, referral to deeper investigation. Even here, the tone is less dramatic than many imagine. It is a negotiation of evidence, numbers, and interpretations.

The deeper truth is that audits expose a philosophical divide. Business owners often see tax as narrative: *I worked hard, I deserve fair recognition.* Tax authorities see it as arithmetic: *does the number reconcile?* The audit is where these worldviews collide. The outcome is rarely decided by whose worldview is nobler, but by whose records are stronger.

There is also a paradox worth noting. The more transparent and prepared you are, the less persuasive you need to be. An entrepreneur who opens a binder or a digital folder containing every requested document, labelled and dated, speaks louder than one who delivers heartfelt speeches about fairness. Auditors are trained to trust order over rhetoric. The very act of producing clean, complete files communicates competence and reduces suspicion.

Yet even with discipline, audits introduce tension. You may prove every figure, and still the authority might adjust an interpretation. Was that meal a legitimate business expense or a personal outing? Was that contract income deferred correctly or prematurely recognised? These grey zones reveal the limits of documentation: you can present evidence, but interpretation belongs to the authority. This is where appeals and negotiations begin, and where strategy matters as much as compliance.

The unresolved question remains: is it possible to build a system so bulletproof that an audit becomes routine, even trivial? Or will the very nature of taxation—its dependence on judgment, on grey areas, on evolving rules—always preserve an element of uncertainty? Perhaps the only certainty is this: those who rely on persuasion will always be anxious. Those who rely on documentation may still be tested, but they will never be unprepared.

Your evidence file: An audit-binder structure maintained year-round ends debates over intent. Good memos are illustrated with short examples.

The nightmare scenario in an audit is not the discovery of fraud, but the erosion of intent. Numbers without context become suspicious; deductions without explanation look opportunistic. An expense claimed for a client dinner may be genuine, but absent notes, it risks being recast as personal indulgence. A payment to a subcontractor may be perfectly legitimate, yet without a contract copy or receipt, it invites speculation. Time and again, disputes hinge not on whether money moved, but on why. The paradox is stark: a business can operate honestly, yet lose credibility simply for failing to preserve its story.

The simplest antidote is also the most overlooked—a deliberately structured *evidence file.* Not a shoebox of receipts nor a scatter of digital folders, but a curated binder, physical or virtual, maintained with the discipline of an annual diary. Its purpose is not merely storage, but defence. Each entry tells a narrative: not just the raw transaction, but the intent, the context, and the trail of supporting documents. In doing so, it transforms what might have been a heated argument into a matter of quick verification.

At its core, the evidence file is built on the principle of traceability. Every material transaction, from the recurring rent payment to the one-off marketing campaign, has a corresponding record. Bank statements link to invoices; invoices are annotated with purpose; anomalous entries are paired with a memo. The audit, in this light, ceases to be a theatre of persuasion. It becomes an exercise in matching tabs to questions, dates to forms. The file speaks, and it speaks consistently.

A well-constructed audit binder typically follows a year's chronology but is subdivided by category—income, direct costs, overheads, taxes. Within each section, order reigns. Receipts are logged alongside corresponding payments, payroll records are reconciled against filings, and contracts sit beside related invoices. The binder is not a catch-all archive but a carefully pruned tree, with branches designed to guide an outsider from root to leaf. The goal is clarity for someone who knows nothing of your business, yet must be convinced that its financial representations are sound.

Consider the power of a short memo. A cryptic expense entry labelled "£425 – conference" raises eyebrows. But attach a one-sentence note—"Industry summit, Manchester, 14 May, attended with prospective clients X and Y"—and the ambiguity evaporates. Similarly, a subcontractor payment accompanied by a signed agreement and evidence of deliverables withstands scrutiny that might otherwise escalate. These memos need not be verbose. In fact, brevity is strength. A single line that captures the *why* preserves intent long after memory fades.

There is a philosophical dimension here. Records without narrative are brittle. They prove what happened but not why it mattered. Narrative without records is equally fragile, reduced to unverifiable testimony. The evidence file unites the two—fact and context—creating a structure resilient to doubt. In this sense, it is less a bureaucratic burden than an extension of memory, a prosthetic for intent.

Examples illustrate the difference. One entrepreneur, audited over a string of travel expenses, had only credit card statements to hand. Every meal appeared identical: restaurant names, dates, amounts. The auditor questioned them as personal. Contrast this with another business that filed each receipt with a note—"client strategy dinner," "supplier negotiation." The first faced disallowances and penalties; the second closed the audit in weeks. The monetary difference was substantial, but the psychological difference was greater: one endured suspicion, the other demonstrated trustworthiness.

Technology has made this discipline easier. Digital tools can capture receipts, tag them with categories, and link them to bank feeds. Yet the technology does not replace judgment. It is the human choice—to write the memo, to group the files, to maintain order—that gives meaning to the archive. The binder is not simply data storage; it is a framework of intent curated with care.

Sceptics may argue that such rigour is overkill, that few audits descend into such detail. But here lies the trap. Audit selection is probabilistic, and once chosen, there is no predicting the depth of inquiry. By the time the letter arrives, it is too late to recreate context. Memory blurs, staff leave, clients move on. The binder is an insurance policy against forgetfulness. It is a discipline that turns uncertainty into readiness.

The deeper lesson extends beyond audits. A business that maintains an evidence file year-round operates with sharper self-awareness. Decisions become easier to review; anomalies are flagged early; financial narratives emerge with coherence. Even absent an audit, the binder becomes a management tool, a mirror reflecting the health and integrity of operations.

And yet, a question lingers. In a world increasingly automated, with AI tools categorising transactions and tax authorities linking directly to bank feeds, will the need for human-annotated evidence fade? Or will the discipline of context remain irreplaceable—the one human element that algorithms cannot infer? Perhaps the future of audit readiness will not abolish the binder but transform it, from a physical folder on a shelf to a living system of structured intent, blending automation with human judgment. Until then, the most resilient defence remains simple: build the file, write the memo, preserve the story.

When to concede, when to appeal: A decision matrix weighs costs, time, and precedent. The goal is to preserve relationships, cash, and focus.

The hardest decision in an audit is not providing the documents, nor surviving the scrutiny. It is deciding whether to stand your ground or to yield. A paradox confronts every business owner: sometimes the truth is on your side, yet the wiser move is to concede; sometimes the claim is flimsy or unfair, but the stakes demand an appeal. The line between pragmatism and principle is thin, and crossing it in the wrong direction can drain not only cash but reputation and attention.

Consider the case of a mid-sized technology consultancy that found itself challenged on its R&D tax credit. The firm had meticulously documented its qualifying projects, but the tax authority argued that routine software upgrades had been misclassified. The partners were certain of their position and had legal opinion to support them. Yet the cost of appeal would have been significant, involving specialist barristers, months of delay, and reputational risk with regulators they would need to engage again in the future. They made the difficult call to concede, writing off the disallowed credit. The decision was not about right and wrong but about focus: they chose growth and client trust over courtroom vindication.

In contrast, a family-run manufacturer was flagged for VAT irregularities when it imported raw materials. Customs authorities insisted duties had been underpaid, but the evidence file proved otherwise. The company weighed the numbers: the disputed amount was modest, but conceding would set a dangerous precedent. If they accepted fault where none existed, future shipments might trigger repeat challenges. They appealed, not because of the immediate sum, but to prevent the erosion of their standing. It was a longer path, but it safeguarded their credibility in cross-border trade.

The art here lies in building a decision matrix, a tool that brings structure to moments of stress. The matrix weighs three elements: cost, time, and precedent. Cost is obvious—what is the financial exposure, including legal fees, lost management hours, and penalties? Time asks a subtler question: how long will this consume leadership energy, and what opportunities will slip while the audit drags on? Precedent, however, is the most underestimated dimension. Does conceding establish a pattern that might haunt you later? Does appealing create a record that strengthens your future resilience? These questions resist spreadsheets alone; they demand judgement sharpened by both numbers and narrative.

There is also the matter of relationships. Tax authorities, auditors, and regulators are not faceless bureaucracies but systems staffed by people. Conceding gracefully can build goodwill, signalling respect for the process. Digging in unnecessarily can sour interactions for years. Conversely, mounting a well-prepared appeal, argued on facts rather than emotion, can earn respect even when the outcome is uncertain. The decision is less about pleasing the individual auditor and more about shaping the long-term tenor of the relationship between your business and the institution.

Some founders err towards over-defence. Pride in their work makes them unwilling to concede even the smallest point, as though acceptance equates to dishonesty. Yet this approach risks turning every audit into protracted conflict. Others swing too far in the opposite direction, conceding readily to preserve peace. In doing so, they invite repeated challenges, appearing as easy targets. The wisest learn to distinguish between symbolic battles worth fighting and tactical retreats that preserve strength.

Philosophically, this balance resembles a lesson from strategy: victory is not defined by winning every skirmish, but by sustaining the capacity to pursue one's larger mission. The point of running a business is not to triumph over tax inspectors; it is to generate value, create livelihoods, and grow. The decision to appeal or concede must always be framed within that broader mission.

The evidence file, discussed earlier, is central to this calculus. Without documentation, appeal is folly. Persuasion is weak against a paper trail that does not exist. But with strong records, the choice expands: you can fight when precedent demands it, or concede when it does not. The file shifts the dynamic from desperation to deliberation.

Still, an enduring tension remains. How much of one's finite energy should be spent defending the past, and how much should be invested in building the future? No decision matrix, however elegant, fully resolves this question. Each audit brings its own context, personalities, and stakes. The best leaders know when to hold fast and when to fold, guided not by ego but by clarity of purpose.

And so, the lingering question for any business owner under review: when the next letter arrives, will you measure the decision in pounds alone, or will you also weigh the invisible currencies of time, trust, and precedent? The answer may determine not just the outcome of an audit, but the shape of the business that emerges on the other side.

Chapter 11
The Year-End Close and Filing Window

Every culture has its rituals of closure. Farmers once measured their year not by the turning of a calendar but by the moment harvest was brought in and the fields left bare. Scholars in medieval universities marked their progress not by birthdays but by disputations and term-end reckonings. In business, the modern equivalent is the year-end close: that moment when the sprawling chaos of a year's trade is distilled into a single, comprehensible record. It is a pause, a reckoning, and a preparation all at once. And like those older rituals, it is both feared and liberating.

The paradox is plain: deadlines that inspire dread are also the very structures that create freedom. Without fixed corridors for filing, without cut-offs for adjustments, owners would drift in endless uncertainty. Yet because these corridors exist, orientation replaces anxiety. The deadline is not merely an enemy to be outmanoeuvred, but a boundary that sharpens focus. Businesses that embrace this logic find that the year-end, rather than an annual crisis, becomes a predictable choreography: a series of steps that build confidence instead of panic.

Consider a small design agency facing its first true filing window. Its founder spent December haunted by imagined disasters—missed deadlines, punitive fines, hostile letters. But when the accountant walked her through a backward plan—marking each critical corridor on a wall calendar—her dread dissolved into clarity. Extensions were not mysterious favours but tools built into the system. Deadlines, once feared, became coordinates in a map she could follow. That shift, from nebulous anxiety to structured orientation, is the essence of year-end mastery.

But deadlines are only one layer of the work. The close is also a time of judgement: which receivables to treat as doubtful, which expenses to accrue, which allowances to invoke. These decisions, seemingly technical, ripple into tax outcomes, cashflow strategies, and investor confidence. To write off a lingering debt is not just an accounting entry but an admission that energy is better spent on the future than chasing the past. To elect a specific allowance is to make a statement about how the business positions itself for opportunity. These are not mechanical moves but acts of stewardship.

Owner compensation and retirement contributions add another layer of nuance. Here, year-end decisions intersect with personal thresholds: income bands, pension caps, and contribution limits that can tilt tax burdens dramatically. A founder who treats December pay as routine salary may miss the chance to optimise; one who aligns it with retirement vehicles and thresholds can shift outcomes for years ahead. The dialogue between business and personal finance is most intense at the close of the year, when the numbers become not just abstract balances but tangible implications for household security and future planning.

Yet all this effort risks being wasted if it evaporates in January amnesia. Too often, the labour of the close is left unarchived, forcing founders and accountants to reconstruct decisions months later with fragments of memory and scattered emails. The antidote is deceptively simple: a tidy package. A closing checklist that collates the trial balance, reconciliations, supporting invoices, and a one-page summary does more than prevent errors—it builds continuity. It ensures that the lessons of one year are the launchpad for the next. Businesses that master this discipline rarely repeat mistakes, because their past decisions remain legible.

The year-end close, then, is not just a compliance ritual. It is a mirror held up to the business, demanding clarity, judgement, and discipline. It compresses a year's complexity into a few decisive moves, forces owners to engage with the interplay between business and personal priorities, and embeds a record that outlasts memory.

The question that lingers is not whether the close will come—it always will—but whether one will arrive at it as a flustered bystander or as a deliberate participant. For those willing to see deadlines as coordinates, adjustments as strategy, and packaging as continuity, the year-end becomes more than an obligation. It becomes an instrument of foresight. The pages ahead will map this instrument, showing how to transform the season of anxiety into a season of control. The test is whether the reader will use it merely to meet obligations, or to turn the year-end into a vantage point from which the next twelve months look not daunting, but already half-won.

Deadlines that matter: Filing corridors and extensions are mapped with a backward plan from due dates. Orientation replaces anxiety.

The curious thing about deadlines is that while they appear fixed and unforgiving, they are also among the few constants that offer security. To many founders and professionals, the word "deadline" summons dread—an invisible guillotine hanging over a venture, ready to strike with penalties and late fees. Yet ask any seasoned operator what keeps them calm in the storm of financial administration, and you will hear the same paradox: deadlines, properly understood, are not the enemy but the map. They are not a trap laid by tax authorities, but coordinates in a terrain that is entirely navigable once you know the paths.

Consider a small consultancy in its third year of operation. Its founder kept stumbling into last-minute scrambles every April, rifling through paper files and pleading with an accountant days before tax season shut. The stress was consuming, the errors costly. Then, one January, she sat down not with tax codes but with a simple calendar. Working backwards from the known filing deadline, she plotted reminders, checkpoints, and contingency markers. Instead of drifting toward chaos, she walked a visible corridor. That year, for the first time, she submitted her return early—and discovered the most surprising part of all: clarity replaced dread, and the once-feared filing season felt almost anticlimactic.

Deadlines matter not because they are imposed, but because they impose orientation. A backward plan transforms amorphous pressure into defined steps. Imagine a marathon without mile markers: even the strongest runners would misjudge their pace, unsure whether to sprint or conserve energy. Filing corridors serve the same purpose. They divide the journey into intervals—quarterly estimates, reconciliations, interim reports—that signal where you stand and how far you must go. Miss the markers, and the final sprint becomes overwhelming. Respect them, and the race itself feels manageable.

In practical terms, the backward plan means beginning with the statutory due date—whether that is 31 January in the UK for self-assessment, 15 April in the United States, or varying corporate deadlines elsewhere—and working in reverse. Several weeks prior, ensure the draft accounts are reconciled. Weeks before that, capture year-end adjustments. Even earlier, confirm all receipts and invoices are logged. Each step is a buffer that prevents bottlenecks. When applied with discipline, this method shrinks the sense of a single terrifying deadline into a chain of smaller, achievable ones.

Extensions, often misunderstood, are not loopholes but pressure valves. To the uninitiated, applying for extra time appears to be an admission of failure or weakness. In reality, most tax authorities design extension corridors deliberately, recognising that complexity is not always resolvable in rigid cycles. Used wisely, extensions preserve accuracy without forfeiting compliance. They should not be treated as excuses for procrastination, but as tools for preserving sanity and precision when legitimate obstacles arise. The lesson is not that extensions absolve disorganisation, but that they form part of the system's rhythm—an official acknowledgement that orientation matters more than heroics.

What makes deadlines psychologically powerful is their capacity to convert infinite possibility into bounded choice. When everything feels possible, procrastination thrives; when time is framed, priorities emerge. This is not merely an administrative truth but a human one. We tend to mistake freedom as the absence of boundaries, when in practice freedom often emerges within boundaries. Filing deadlines illustrate this with brutal clarity: those who respect them find more energy for creativity, because compliance no longer devours their attention. Those who resist them often drown in preventable emergencies.

It is worth acknowledging, too, that deadlines serve another invisible role: they align the business with its stakeholders. Banks, investors, regulators, and even employees draw confidence not from promises but from proof of timely reporting. When returns are filed on schedule, when documents are orderly, when extensions are requested transparently, the signal is one of control. A missed deadline, by contrast, casts a shadow longer than the fine—it implies negligence, unreliability, or fragility in the system. The financial cost of lateness is often dwarfed by the reputational one.

Yet the most profound insight is this: deadlines are not fixed only in relation to government calendars. They can be reframed within the business itself. A founder who decides that all records will be reconciled monthly, that anomalies will be flagged within forty-eight hours, and that a file will be packaged by mid-January has created internal deadlines that make statutory ones trivial. The official corridor ceases to be the starting point and becomes instead a final, formal step in a much longer choreography. By taking control of time, the founder reclaims control of attention.

The paradox remains unresolved: deadlines feel oppressive, yet they liberate; they seem external, yet they can be internalised; they threaten anxiety, yet they create orientation. The businesses that learn to work with this paradox discover that the year-end no longer looms like a cliff. It arrives as a crossing point already rehearsed, already mapped. The real question is whether we will continue treating deadlines as an adversary to evade—or whether we might instead recognise them as a scaffold that, if embraced, makes clarity not just possible, but inevitable.

Final adjustments: accruals, write-offs, allowances: Year-end clean-ups and elections improve clarity, translating accounting moves into tax effects

Every system of record-keeping, from the wax tablets of Mesopotamia to the cloud dashboards of today, carries with it a problem: the year does not end when the clock strikes midnight on 31 December, or 31 March, or any other chosen date. Invoices remain unpaid, assets decline in usefulness, debts linger in grey zones. The business world does not conform neatly to the tax calendar, and so accounting must intervene with adjustments—

devices that close the gap between the living rhythm of commerce and the artificial cut-off of reporting seasons. What seems like technical minutiae—accruals, write-offs, allowances—turns out to be the hinge on which truth, trust, and tax all swing.

Take the example of a manufacturer in Leeds whose books showed healthy profits in December, only for January to bring a flood of supplier invoices for materials used in November. Without accrual adjustments, the year-end profit was inflated, painting a false picture to shareholders and the tax authority alike. Conversely, another firm in Toronto carried a client receivable on its books long past collectability, refusing to acknowledge it as a write-off. The numbers looked stronger on paper than reality would allow—until an audit forced a correction, damaging credibility. These stories illustrate why the year-end close is not just a compliance exercise but an act of intellectual honesty: to acknowledge costs when they are incurred, income when it is earned, and losses when they are unavoidable.

Accruals are perhaps the most misunderstood of the adjustments. They are not optional embellishments but necessary bridges between timing mismatches. Salaries earned in December but paid in January must be recorded in the period when employees performed the work; utilities consumed but not yet billed must also appear. Without this matching principle, financial statements devolve into arbitrary cash snapshots, useless for decision-making and misleading for tax assessments. The accrual, then, is not merely an accounting technique—it is an assertion that obligations and entitlements exist independent of the speed at which money moves.

Write-offs, by contrast, demand a different kind of discipline: the willingness to admit that not all promises of payment will be fulfilled. For many entrepreneurs, writing off a receivable feels like conceding defeat, as though persistence might still conjure recovery. Yet keeping dead debts alive distorts both tax liability and business planning. A timely write-off recognises that losses are as real as gains, and that acknowledging them sooner allows for a truer recalibration of resources. The lesson is stark but liberating: honesty about what is unrecoverable clears the path for new growth.

Allowances add nuance by accepting that not all uncertainty can be resolved with a binary answer. Whereas a write-off says, "this debt is gone," an allowance for doubtful accounts concedes, "some portion of these debts may fail." The same principle applies to inventory obsolescence or warranty obligations. Rather than waiting for losses to materialise, the allowance anticipates them, tempering optimism with prudence. Here lies the philosophical heart of year-end adjustments: they acknowledge that business operates in probabilities, not certainties, and that responsible stewardship means recognising risk even before it crystallises.

These adjustments also translate directly into *tax effects*. An unaccrued expense inflates profit, increasing taxable income prematurely. A failure to record allowances can deny deductions until losses become undeniable, often years later. Conversely, aggressive write-offs may invite challenge from authorities who see them as premature. Each adjustment, therefore, sits at the intersection of accounting judgment and tax consequence. It is not enough to know the rules; one must understand their impact on the flow of cash, compliance, and reputation.

Yet there is another dimension to these year-end clean-ups: they are not only about accuracy, but about agency. Businesses often face elections—choices about depreciation methods, timing of allowances, or the recognition of certain accruals—that carry strategic weight. Choosing to accelerate depreciation may lower current tax but reduce future deductions. Deferring an allowance may improve short-term optics but create exposure later. These elections are not clerical; they are moments where management articulates its priorities, trading between present and future, between cash and clarity.

What makes these final adjustments fascinating is the way they bind the technical to the human. Behind each accrual lies a decision about fairness to employees or suppliers. Behind each write-off lies the recognition of fallibility—an admission that not all ventures succeed. Behind each allowance lies humility, a willingness to accept uncertainty as inherent to enterprise. These are not simply debits and credits; they are reflections of how a business confronts time, risk, and truth.

There is also a subtle cultural pattern here: some organisations treat year-end adjustments as a grudging necessity, left to accountants in the last week of filing. Others embrace them as an annual ritual of clarity, a moment to reset narratives and confront reality head-on. The latter tend to emerge stronger, not because they minimise tax more effectively, but because they cultivate resilience. They understand that clean books are not just compliant books—they are strategic tools that allow leadership to see clearly and act decisively.

The paradox is that these adjustments, though they live in footnotes and working papers, wield influence disproportionate to their apparent size. A missed accrual can change profit trends, mislead investors, or trigger regulatory scrutiny. A neglected write-off can inflate valuation during a financing round, only to collapse trust later. An overlooked allowance can leave a company scrambling when risks mature. In other words, the smallest year-end entries can reshape the largest strategic decisions.

The tension, then, is not whether to make these adjustments—they are unavoidable—but how to approach them: as perfunctory chores, or as deliberate acts of integrity and foresight. Each year-end offers a choice: to tidy the numbers superficially, or to engage seriously with the underlying economic realities. The question that remains is whether leaders will seize that chance for clarity—or defer it, hoping the distortions can be postponed another year. The answer, as always, will be written not only in the accounts but in the trajectory of the business itself.

Owner pay and retirement contributions: Compensation interacts with thresholds and retirement vehicles; notes point to common options without prescribing

Few decisions test the balance between today's needs and tomorrow's security quite like how an owner chooses to pay themselves. It is deceptively simple on the surface—money leaves the business and lands in the owner's pocket—but beneath that movement lie layers of thresholds, incentives, and trade-offs that ripple through tax, retirement planning, and even perceptions of the business's stability. To underpay is to risk personal strain and underfunded retirement; to overpay is to drain working capital and miss opportunities for tax-efficient structuring. Every line drawn on the payslip reflects a philosophy of how the present negotiates with the future.

Consider the founder of a consulting firm in London. In her second year, she debated whether to take a higher salary or keep her compensation low and instead contribute more to her pension scheme. A higher salary improved her mortgage prospects but exposed her to a higher income tax band. By contrast, pension contributions reduced her taxable income and built long-term security, yet they locked away funds she might need if the business faltered. Neither option was strictly "right." What mattered was recognising that compensation is not just a transfer—it is a strategic lever.

Thresholds sit at the centre of this calculation. Every jurisdiction creates invisible cliffs—points where a pound or dollar more in income tips the balance into a new tax rate, alters eligibility for credits, or caps retirement contributions. In the United States, self-employment income above certain thresholds opens doors to tax-advantaged retirement plans like the SEP IRA or Solo 401(k), while simultaneously triggering higher Medicare surcharges. In the UK, exceeding the £100,000 adjusted net income threshold gradually removes the personal allowance, effectively creating a hidden marginal rate of over 60%. In India, employee provident fund rules, section 80C deductions, and voluntary pension options intersect in ways that shape take-home pay just as much as gross salary does. These thresholds are not quirks—they are pressure points where owners must decide whether to push forward, hold back, or redirect compensation into retirement vehicles.

The vehicles themselves embody different philosophies of time. A traditional pension, with its lockbox of deferred gratification, rewards patience and compound growth. Employer-sponsored accounts, whether a Canadian RRSP or a UK workplace pension, offer tax relief at entry but limit liquidity. Defined contribution plans emphasise flexibility but also shift investment risk squarely onto the individual. For business owners, the menu is broader but the choices are starker: pay today as salary, dividend, or bonus—or siphon into retirement accounts that may yield decades of tax efficiency but at the cost of immediate control.

There is also the interplay between *personal* thresholds and *business* dynamics. High owner pay may reassure lenders that the business generates sustainable profits, but it may simultaneously increase payroll taxes or reduce retained earnings that could be reinvested. Conversely, lean owner pay may signal reinvestment discipline but can raise eyebrows with tax authorities who scrutinise "reasonable compensation" rules in certain jurisdictions. In Canada and the US especially, the distinction between salary and dividend is not cosmetic: it alters the burden of social security contributions, access to retirement contributions, and the timing of personal tax liability.

Examples abound of owners navigating these crossroads. A software entrepreneur in Bangalore shifted from a modest salary supplemented by dividend payouts to a more structured package once venture capital arrived, ensuring predictable personal cash flow while preserving investor confidence. A family-owned manufacturing firm in Ohio deliberately set owner salaries just below a key Medicare threshold, diverting the excess into retirement plans. Meanwhile, a London-based creative agency kept owner compensation low during growth years but maxed out pension allowances annually, turning tax relief into a form of deferred self-compensation that would smooth future volatility.

Philosophically, the tension lies in how we conceive of "enough." Owner pay decisions often expose the gap between lifestyle consumption and long-term stewardship. Retirement contributions, though framed as financial vehicles, are also acts of humility: a recognition that future needs deserve as much attention as present desires. Setting aside earnings for decades hence is a kind of dialogue with one's future self—a commitment that goes beyond compliance into questions of identity, responsibility, and resilience.

There is also a collective dimension. For employees, seeing the owner participate in retirement savings schemes can signal confidence and solidarity, encouraging uptake and strengthening workplace culture. For regulators, clear distinctions between salary, dividends, and pension contributions reduce suspicion of manipulation. For the owner's family, the decisions shape not only current household income but also the security of future inheritances. These choices therefore carry weight beyond balance sheets—they ripple into trust, morale, and reputation.

And yet, the paradox remains: the most "rational" decision is rarely absolute. It depends on age, growth stage, jurisdiction, appetite for liquidity, and the owner's personal definition of security. A forty-year-old founder might prioritise retirement contributions aggressively, seeing them as compounders. A sixty-year-old owner planning succession may favour higher pay today to meet lifestyle goals before transition. The decision matrix is less about discovering one perfect formula and more about understanding the trade-offs clearly enough to choose deliberately.

At year-end, when adjustments crystallise into filings, these choices reveal themselves most starkly. Owners who have navigated thresholds thoughtfully see tax efficiency and retirement readiness align. Those who drift without a framework often discover they have paid more tax than necessary or underfunded their future. The act of calibrating owner pay and retirement contributions is not just a technical duty; it is a narrative about how the business honours both its present vitality and its future obligations.

The open question is whether owners will continue to treat compensation as a static draw, or whether they will reframe it as a strategic design—one that balances cash, tax, and time with the same rigour they bring to products and markets. It is in this reframing that clarity is won and anxiety fades. The challenge, then, is simple but profound: how deliberately will you pay yourself?

Packaging the file: A closing checklist produces a complete archive and a one-page summary for next year, preventing January amnesia

Every January, accountants and business owners alike confront the same frustration: the fog of forgetting. Twelve months of invoices, receipts, adjustments, and explanations collapse into a single question—*what happened last year?* Projects blur, decisions lose their context, and the narrative of a company's financial life risks being rewritten from scraps. This phenomenon, call it "January amnesia," is not caused by negligence but by the sheer velocity of business. The problem is not only one of memory but of structure. Without a deliberate archive, the year-end story becomes guesswork.

Now consider the contrasting picture: a meticulously packaged year-end file, complete with reconciliations, supporting documents, and a crisp one-page summary. The difference is palpable. Instead of combing through inboxes and folders, the owner begins the year with a compass—last year's course charted clearly, ready to inform this year's strategy. The act of closing is not simply a compliance exercise but an investment in clarity, efficiency, and foresight. A well-packaged file transforms the year-end from a frantic scramble into a disciplined ritual, protecting both the present filing and the future review.

What makes such a file powerful is its dual purpose: to satisfy external scrutiny while equipping internal decision-making. Tax authorities, auditors, or investors see accuracy and organisation; owners and managers see patterns, lessons, and direction. It is both shield and map. Without it, errors multiply: unclaimed deductions vanish, duplicated expenses sneak through, and mismatched reports raise red flags. With it, the business speaks in a single, coherent voice.

At the heart of this process is the checklist. Checklists, though deceptively simple, are one of the most potent tools in human history for reducing error. Surgeons, pilots, and engineers rely on them because memory is fallible under pressure. Business owners are no different. The checklist for year-end—trial balances reconciled, ageing reports reviewed, invoices matched, accruals adjusted, write-offs documented—removes ambiguity and creates accountability. Nothing is left to improvisation. Each tick marks not only a completed task but a layer of resilience.

Take the example of a mid-sized design agency. In its early years, filing season meant chaos: scattered receipts, undocumented loans from directors, and unresolved entries left hanging in the general ledger. The first tax filing cost weeks of stress and thousands in accountant fees. By its fifth year, the agency had introduced a closing checklist. Every December, staff gathered supporting documents, flagged anomalies, and produced a one-page narrative of the year: major client wins, large capital purchases, debt repayments, and payroll shifts. When the accountant received the file, the audit trail was clear. Fees dropped, errors shrank, and decision-making sharpened because the business itself understood its own story.

There is also a philosophical elegance in packaging the file. It forces a business to confront its year honestly, without revisionism. Numbers, when properly archived, resist the human tendency to misremember or rationalise. That investment you thought was minor turns out to be the year's largest outlay. That "temporary" loan from the director's account has lingered for three quarters. The checklist, and the archive it produces, is a mirror. It does not flatter, but it clarifies. And clarity is what turns financial data into insight.

The one-page summary, in particular, deserves emphasis. Complexity is captured, but then distilled. This document is not for regulators—it is for the owner, the future self who will need to recall quickly what mattered. It might note: "Year marked by expansion into new market; payroll rose 15%; large equipment purchase financed via loan; deferred revenue increased; pension contributions maxed." In five bullet points, the past is secured against the erosion of memory. It is, in effect, a letter from one year's management team to the next, ensuring continuity in vision and action.

Packaging the file is not a clerical chore; it is an act of stewardship. It creates continuity across years, reduces reliance on individual memory, and elevates financial records from raw data to a coherent narrative. It also protects focus: the fewer surprises unearthed in March or April, the more energy can be directed towards strategy rather than crisis management.

Yet the unresolved tension lingers. Despite the clear benefits, many owners neglect this discipline until an audit looms or a loan application demands detail. The question is not whether packaging the file matters—it unquestionably does—but whether businesses will make it a standing ritual, woven into the rhythm of each December, rather than a reactive scramble when stakes are high. To answer that question is to decide whether next January begins with confusion or with clarity.

Chapter 12
Planning Windows You Can Actually Use

There is a strange paradox at the heart of financial planning. On the one hand, the calendar is fixed: tax deadlines arrive the same time each year, quarterly filings do not move, and annual accounts must always be signed. Yet within this rigid structure, fortunes are made or lost by those who recognise that timing is not just constraint but opportunity. A single decision—when to invoice a client, when to purchase equipment, when to shift an ownership structure—can transform a tax bill or cash position more dramatically than months of incremental tweaks. Planning, then, is less about a constant vigilance of minor adjustments and more about knowing which windows matter, and being ready to act when they open.

Consider the difference between the entrepreneur who treats tax as an afterthought and the one who builds it into every decision. The first sets prices, pays staff, and hopes the leftovers cover the revenue authority. The second integrates tax into the very fabric of pricing and cash-flow planning, recognising that a one- or two-percent margin adjustment can quietly fund liabilities without stress. What looks to the outside observer like the same business is, in reality, two different organisms: one perpetually firefighting, the other steadily compounding strength through foresight.

Yet planning windows are often misunderstood. The temptation is to manufacture complexity, to spin artificial gymnastics at year-end in the hope of shaving points from a tax bill. But high-impact planning is usually simple and rare: the well-timed purchase before year-end, the choice to delay or accelerate invoicing by a few weeks, the restructuring of an entity at the point growth demands it. These are infrequent but powerful interventions. They require preparation, but they do not demand constant tinkering. The art lies not in doing more but in knowing when to move and when to stand still.

For those expanding across borders, the stakes multiply. What begins as a new market can quickly become a web of withholding taxes, platform rules, and consumer levies. Many founders find themselves improvising until the complexity catches up with them. A checklist—practical, bounded, and deliberately minimal—becomes the difference between sustainable growth and costly missteps. Cross-border strategy should invite complexity only when it genuinely adds value, not when it is simply the by-product of neglect.

The discipline that ties all this together is the calendar. Not the sprawling wall chart littered with notes, but the pared-down, durable system that reduces overwhelm to habit: weekly reviews of cash and obligations, monthly reconciliations, quarterly set-asides and filings. This one-page calendar becomes an operating system for the financial life of a business. It orients the owner, replaces anxiety with rhythm, and ensures that when a planning window opens, the business is not caught flat-footed but prepared to step through it.

What follows in this chapter is not a set of tricks or evasions. It is a reorientation towards planning as something durable, calm, and integrated. The aim is not to outsmart the tax code with clever stunts, but to align decisions—pricing, spending, structuring—with the natural rhythm of deadlines and opportunities. The question is not whether the calendar will govern your business; it already does. The question is whether you will let it be an adversary, springing traps and surprises, or whether you will make it an ally, a frame that quietly preserves cash, reduces stress, and amplifies outcomes. The choice, as ever, belongs to those willing to prepare.

Price, profit, and tax as one calculation: Tax set-asides are integrated into pricing and cash-flow planning. Small margin changes can fund taxes without stress.

Imagine a business owner who proudly declares a year of record sales, only to end up scrambling to cover a tax bill that wipes out their apparent success. The paradox is familiar: profit on paper can coexist with anxiety in practice. The culprit is not the tax code itself but a fragmented way of thinking. Price, profit, and tax are treated as separate domains—pricing as a market play, profit as operational discipline, and tax as an unwelcome afterthought. Yet when considered together, as one seamless calculation, these forces align into a system that funds itself.

Consider the restaurateur who sets menu prices by intuition, rounding numbers to "what feels right" rather than calculating margins with taxes in mind. At the end of the year, despite full tables, they find their cash flow thin and their liabilities daunting. Contrast this with the proprietor who integrates tax into pricing from the outset. A small upward adjustment of two per cent on each dish—barely noticed by customers—creates a steady stream of set-aside funds. For one, tax is a stress-inducing lump sum; for the other, it is already prepaid by the logic of the business itself. The lesson is simple but profound: taxes do not become unbearable when planned for in fractions; they become unbearable when ignored until they arrive as a whole.

This integration begins with mindset. Too many owners treat tax as an external imposition, detached from the "real" performance of the business. But in reality, tax is not separate from profit—it is a share of it. Once this truth is accepted, the decision to build set-asides into every transaction becomes obvious. A sale is not fully complete until the tax portion is acknowledged and ringfenced. The business that internalises this creates stability not through clever tricks but through honest arithmetic applied consistently.

The mechanics can be surprisingly straightforward. Suppose a consultancy charges £1,000 for a service. If their after-expense profit margin is 30%, they keep £300. Tax obligations might consume £60 to £90 of this, depending on jurisdiction. Many owners treat the £300 as theirs and worry about tax later, only to discover that their net position is closer to £210. A different approach is to price the service at £1,030, building in the tax set-aside invisibly, or to discipline themselves to allocate £90 immediately upon receipt. In either case, the "profit" felt in the moment is aligned with the "profit" that survives the return. Illusions of abundance are replaced with clarity of means.

The resistance to this approach often stems from fear of pricing. Owners worry that passing costs to customers will reduce competitiveness. Yet the empirical reality is that marginal increases—fractions of a pound, a few percentage points—rarely deter the right buyers. What drives purchasing decisions is value perception, not microscopic pricing differences. More importantly, underpricing to avoid discomfort guarantees erosion: the business underfunds itself, starves its reserves, and bleeds stress into every cycle. By contrast, pricing with tax in mind honours the real cost of delivering value, signalling to customers that they are dealing with a sustainable, confident enterprise.

The implications extend beyond numbers. Integrating tax into pricing fosters a culture of foresight. Teams learn that every sale is not just revenue but obligation and opportunity. They understand that the company's health is measured not only by what comes in but also by what is responsibly set aside. This shifts the psychology of operations from reactive to anticipatory. Instead of tax season being a dreaded disruption, it becomes a checkpoint passed with calm.

There is also philosophical depth here. At its heart, integrating tax into pricing is an act of honesty—both with oneself and with the marketplace. It acknowledges the inevitability of shared obligations in society and refuses to indulge in the illusion that one can consume today without settling accounts tomorrow. This honesty creates freedom: the owner who faces tax directly is paradoxically less burdened than the one who tries to ignore it. The former experiences tax as routine, built into the flow of operations. The latter experiences it as shock, perpetually arriving at the worst possible time.

Case studies reinforce the point. A design agency that implemented a 5% "tax buffer" on every invoice found that, within a year, they had not only eliminated tax stress but also created a small surplus that funded strategic investments. A craft manufacturer, by contrast, resisted raising prices, clinging to razor-thin margins. When tax bills arrived, they borrowed at punitive rates to cover them. One business treated tax as part of the arithmetic of value; the other treated it as an external nuisance. Their divergent outcomes stemmed from this single difference in orientation.

Of course, integration does not mean overcomplication. Businesses need not produce labyrinthine models to calculate tax exposure with microscopic precision. Simplicity often works best: fixed set-aside percentages, consistent with local tax brackets, applied automatically through accounting software or bank rules. The genius lies not in granular exactitude but in building a system that operates invisibly, leaving the owner free to focus on value creation.

The broader insight is that small adjustments, consistently applied, accumulate into profound advantages. Just as compound interest turns modest savings into wealth, compound discipline turns small price changes into resilience. The question for any owner, then, is not whether they can afford to integrate tax into pricing, but whether they can afford not to.

And yet, one tension remains. If tax is seamlessly integrated into pricing, should customers ever be made aware of it? Some argue for transparency—itemising tax burdens to highlight the cost of compliance. Others argue for discretion—baking it invisibly into prices to preserve simplicity. Both approaches carry implications for trust, perception, and brand identity. The answer is contextual, but the deeper lesson is constant: whether visible or invisible, tax must be present in the arithmetic. Ignoring it is not an option.

Perhaps the final paradox is this: by treating tax as inseparable from price and profit, business owners do not diminish their enterprise but enlarge it. They move from anxiety to orientation, from surprise to control. And in doing so, they discover that the difference between stress and sustainability is often measured in the smallest of margins—the kind no customer notices, but every owner feels. The real question is whether one dares to shift perspective and accept that price, profit, and tax were never separate to begin with.

Big moves, small windows: Few, high-impact windows—timed purchases, billing shifts, entity changes—are paired with cautions against artificial gymnastics.

History is filled with turning points where timing, rather than sheer effort, determined the outcome. A treaty signed one day later, a trade executed one hour earlier, a decision deferred until the season turned—each instance reminds us that leverage is often a matter of *when*, not simply *what.* In finance and taxation, the same principle applies. The year-end window, the quarterly filing cut-off, the moment of incorporation or restructuring—these are not trivial dates in a calendar but thresholds where large outcomes hinge on small, deliberate moves.

Consider the case of a small software firm debating whether to purchase key equipment in December or January. On the surface, the difference is negligible; the computers will perform the same tasks regardless of delivery date. Yet for the company's tax liability, the timing determines whether depreciation begins this year or the next, shaping cash flow for months to come. What looks like an administrative detail is, in fact, a decision worth thousands. The point is not to dramatise minutiae, but to recognise that certain moments—though rare—carry disproportionate weight.

The disciplined owner, then, does not scatter energy across every conceivable tactic. They identify the *few* high-impact windows that matter and align decisions accordingly. Timing a purchase to bring forward a deduction, shifting billing slightly to smooth revenue recognition, or choosing the precise date for an entity change—each of these is an example of a move that looks modest in isolation but is amplified by the calendar's rules. These are not everyday tricks; they are the rare moments when the structure of law and time intersects with strategy.

The danger, however, lies in mistaking subtle leverage for unlimited opportunity. Tax codes are littered with stories of businesses that stretched timing games too far—deferring revenue in ways that strained credibility, booking phantom expenses, or inventing artificial transactions designed only to reduce liability. What begins as a tactical alignment with legitimate windows can slide into what might be called *artificial gymnastics*: moves that have no economic substance but attempt to exploit rules. The former builds resilience; the latter risks penalties and reputational damage.

A healthier approach begins with restraint. Take billing shifts: a consultancy might bring forward invoicing in December to lock in revenue, or defer slightly to January to ease cash flow and reduce the current year's taxable base. Both can be legitimate, provided they reflect real business activity and client agreement. But when billing becomes a shell game, with invoices created and cancelled only to distort figures, the firm crosses from strategy to artifice. The dividing line is whether the move has economic reality or is purely an accounting illusion.

Entity changes are another powerful but delicate window. Moving from sole proprietorship to limited company, or converting to a partnership, can reshape tax exposure, liability, and funding opportunities. The decision may unlock savings and protections that redefine a business's trajectory. Yet entity changes also carry costs, obligations, and potential future constraints. A limited company may reduce tax in one dimension but complicate personal withdrawals. Timing matters here too: restructuring just before a profitable contract lands may capture significant benefit, but restructuring out of habit or fashion creates needless administrative burden.

These examples highlight a broader truth: the discipline lies not in spotting every possible window but in knowing which are *worth acting upon*. Tax and accounting professionals speak of the "materiality" of decisions—whether the impact is large enough to justify the effort. For small businesses, chasing minor advantages through constant manoeuvring often costs more in distraction and fees than it saves in liability. The wiser path is to focus energy on a handful of pivotal choices each year.

Philosophically, this distinction mirrors a deeper human dilemma: the difference between strategy and cleverness. Strategy is choosing moments of high leverage and acting decisively. Cleverness is scattering effort across countless tricks, many of which backfire or erode credibility. The disciplined owner, like the disciplined strategist, cultivates patience—waiting for the right window and resisting the itch to fabricate opportunities. In this sense, restraint is not passive but active: the refusal to overplay one's hand is itself a form of strength.

Case studies bear this out. A family-owned retailer who timed its major refurbishment in a year of high profits not only secured accelerated deductions but also refreshed its brand ahead of peak season. The move was both economically real and fiscally smart. By contrast, a start-up founder who engaged in complex inter-company invoicing to defer income found themselves facing not only disallowed deductions but also months of distraction defending contrived transactions. One business aligned with reality and magnified its advantage; the other built on illusion and paid the price.

There is also a psychological dividend in narrowing focus to these few windows. Anxiety around tax often stems from the belief that everything matters equally, that every expense must be optimised, every invoice perfectly timed. This mindset creates exhaustion and a false sense of fragility. But when owners recognise that only a handful of decisions truly move the needle, they gain clarity. Planning reduces to a manageable rhythm: a few critical conversations with an accountant, a handful of deliberate moves each year, and otherwise steady operations free of tax acrobatics.

Yet a final tension lingers. If restraint is so important, how does one distinguish between legitimate optimisation and dangerous gymnastics? The line is not always bright. Some jurisdictions tighten rules abruptly, reclassifying what was once acceptable timing as artificial deferral. What is seen as prudent strategy today can be questioned tomorrow. This is why the most resilient approach pairs tactical awareness with conservative framing: make moves that are defensible not only to yourself but to any reasonable outsider. Documentation, clarity of intent, and the alignment of form with substance provide the best defence against shifting rules.

Ultimately, the philosophy of "big moves, small windows" is about leverage and discipline. It asks the owner to respect time as a multiplier of decisions, to act when the calendar amplifies results, and to refrain when the urge to outwit the system tempts them towards fragility. The question that remains is whether business owners can cultivate the patience to wait for those few decisive windows, or whether they will succumb to the restless search for tricks that promise more than they can deliver. In the quiet balance between those choices lies not only tax efficiency but the integrity and resilience of the enterprise itself.

Cross-border sanity: A checklist for platforms, withholding, and consumer taxes keeps growth from outpacing compliance and invites optional complexity only.

The allure of international markets has always carried with it a kind of double-edged promise: expansion and exposure, opportunity and oversight. A small business in London might sell a product to a customer in Berlin, a course to a client in New York, or software access to a subscriber in Singapore—all within a single day, all processed automatically by digital platforms. What looks like seamless borderless commerce on the surface is, beneath the skin, a dense web of obligations, thresholds, and compliance traps that vary by jurisdiction. The paradox is stark: the very platforms that enable effortless global reach also quietly draw owners into tax systems they may not even know they have entered.

Take the case of a design studio that moved into selling digital downloads. Using a popular marketplace, they quickly attracted international buyers. The studio assumed the platform would handle everything, but months later a notice arrived: unpaid VAT in multiple EU countries. The oversight was not malice but a misunderstanding of who, in law, was deemed the seller. The platform had managed payment, but not tax registration or filings. What had been a story of growth turned overnight into a costly lesson in cross-border complexity.

This tension—between ambition and compliance—is not new. Centuries ago, merchants in trading hubs like Venice or Amsterdam faced similar puzzles: where was duty owed, and to whom? But today's problem is accelerated by the invisibility of borders online.

A website does not carry the physical cues of jurisdiction, yet the law insists on drawing its lines. What matters is not where a seller sits but where the buyer is located, where the payment is processed, and sometimes even where the servers run. The modern entrepreneur must therefore adopt a discipline: to treat cross-border commerce not as a tangle of unknowable rules but as a checklist of predictable checkpoints, manageable if approached with clarity.

That checklist begins with platforms. Some marketplaces assume tax responsibility on behalf of sellers, particularly for consumer goods in the EU, the UK, or certain US states. Others merely process payments, leaving the seller fully exposed to VAT, GST, or sales tax obligations. The first discipline is therefore mapping which platforms act as "deemed suppliers" and which simply pass through transactions. This simple distinction can prevent the error of assuming tax is already "taken care of" when in fact it is not.

The second checkpoint is withholding. Cross-border payments, especially for services, are often subject to mandatory deductions before money reaches the seller. A consultant billing a client in India or Brazil may find 10–20% withheld for tax at source, with the possibility of reclaiming part of it only through complex treaty mechanisms. The practical effect is that cash flow shrinks before invoices are even received, often leaving the seller bewildered. The disciplined business anticipates this, checking whether treaties exist, and whether tax identification numbers or certificates are needed to reduce the withholding. Ignorance here is expensive; awareness turns a nasty surprise into a predictable adjustment.

Then comes the third checkpoint: consumer taxes. Unlike corporate taxes, which usually hinge on profit, consumer-facing levies like VAT or GST often apply to the *sale itself*, regardless of margin. A single subscription sold to a German customer may trigger an obligation for VAT reporting, even if the seller is in another continent. Some jurisdictions, like the EU, have introduced thresholds to ease the burden, while others impose obligations from the very first sale. Businesses that scale across borders must therefore recognise that growth can outpace compliance if no monitoring system is in place. It is not unusual for founders to find themselves retroactively liable for thousands in unpaid consumer tax simply because sales in one jurisdiction crept quietly above a filing threshold.

The temptation is to respond to this complexity by either ignoring it entirely or drowning in over-engineering. Both extremes are costly. Ignoring obligations invites penalties and reputational damage, especially when payment processors begin freezing funds due to non-compliance. Over-engineering, on the other hand, saps resources—registering in every jurisdiction, hiring consultants prematurely, and building reporting systems that outstrip actual sales. The balanced approach is to view cross-border compliance as optional complexity, to be taken on only when growth justifies it. The key discipline is sequencing: *expand your compliance footprint only in line with actual sales footprint.*

Here lies the philosophical dimension of cross-border sanity. Expansion is often equated with sophistication, yet maturity lies in restraint. To delay entry into certain markets until infrastructure is ready is not weakness but wisdom. To decline selling in jurisdictions where compliance burdens outweigh benefits is not timidity but strategy. The borderless internet tempts us to think every buyer is within reach; the prudent owner recognises that *not every buyer is worth the cost of access.* Growth is measured not by raw reach but by sustainable participation in markets where rules can be followed with confidence.

Practical examples reinforce the point. A SaaS company that chose to restrict sales temporarily to the UK and US avoided the distraction of EU VAT until its customer base was strong enough to justify proper systems. By contrast, an e-commerce start-up that launched globally on day one spent more on compliance consultants in its first year than on marketing, its ambition devoured by paperwork. In both cases, the revenue was modest, but the discipline—or lack thereof—determined whether growth was supported or strangled.

What emerges is a principle: cross-border expansion is best treated as a staged process, supported by a living checklist. Platforms, withholding, consumer taxes—each item can be clarified in advance, each step scaled when necessary. A one-page document, reviewed quarterly, can provide more resilience than reams of theoretical guidance. It is not glamour but sanity that matters here.

And yet the unresolved tension remains: how far should entrepreneurs go in pursuit of international growth before compliance costs erode the very margins they sought to expand? There is no universal answer, only the reminder that every border crossed carries with it not just opportunity but obligation. The wiser path is not to fear those obligations, nor to dismiss them, but to integrate them into the decision of whether expansion is truly worth it. Growth without compliance is fragility; compliance without growth is waste. The challenge is to walk the narrow path where opportunity and responsibility meet—and to know when to stop.

The durable calendar: A one-page weekly, monthly, and quarterly calendar becomes the operating system for keeping more of what you earn.

It is one of the quietest but most decisive truths of financial life: the difference between those who keep what they earn and those who bleed it away is rarely knowledge, and more often rhythm. A well-structured calendar is not a planner's ornament but a survival tool. Consider the contrast between two owners at year's end: one is scrambling through a half-forgotten email thread for deadlines, fretting over receipts, begging for an extension; the other, calm, flicks open a single sheet of paper—a durable calendar that has been their compass for an entire year. The former lives in reaction, the latter in orientation. Both may have the same intellect and the same accountant, yet their outcomes are worlds apart.

The paradox is this: in a world of infinite apps, digital reminders, and cloud tools, it is often the low-tech, distilled version—a single page—that delivers real mastery. Sophistication does not come from layering systems upon systems, but from paring back until only the essential remains visible. The durable calendar, maintained weekly, monthly, and quarterly, functions as an operating system in the truest sense: it governs when attention is given, and by that governance prevents panic, drift, and waste.

At its core, the calendar is not about compliance alone. It is about mental clarity. Deadlines, once mapped into their rightful corridors, cease to feel like traps and begin to resemble checkpoints. Payments, filings, reviews—what might otherwise come as ambushes arrive instead as rehearsed choreography. The value of this clarity is not merely financial; it is emotional. Anxiety thrives on the unknown. By rendering the year's financial obligations visible and finite, the durable calendar converts dread into discipline.

A weekly rhythm provides the tightest pulse. It might include a Friday review of receipts, a reconciliation of cash inflows, or a quick scan of outstanding invoices. These are not grand tasks but micro-habits, each one designed to prevent January amnesia—the annual fog in which entire months of small decisions vanish without trace. Weekly checkpoints are not about detail but momentum: by maintaining a living pulse, the year never slips too far off track.

Monthly, the view widens. Here is where payroll, VAT filings, and supplier reconciliations take their place. Think of the monthly review as a clearing of the ground, a way of ensuring that every 30 days the business stands on solid footing. Without it, creeping accruals of error turn into crises. With it, corrections are made while they are still cheap, both in money and time. In this sense, the monthly discipline embodies a philosophical truth: prevention is always less costly than cure.

Quarterly, the calendar becomes strategic. This is where estimated tax payments fall, where owners revisit their compensation and retirement contributions, and where profit is assessed not just in the rear-view mirror but as a forward driver. Quarterly checkpoints are the bridges between the daily grind and the annual filing; they stop the year from being experienced as a single overwhelming crunch. They are also moments of reflection—occasions to ask whether the business is merely keeping up, or actually keeping more of what it earns.

The beauty of a one-page format is that it flattens time. Instead of treating deadlines as scattered landmines, the page arranges them in a visible sequence, no longer surprising but anticipated. There is something almost ancient about this discipline: monks once kept their year marked on parchment, not because they lacked technology but because wisdom recognises the power of compression. A single view of the year's obligations gives owners what software rarely does—context.

Yet the calendar is not merely a defensive shield against penalties. It is also an offensive tool for opportunity. By knowing when cash must flow out, one can plan when cash should optimally flow in. By understanding the corridor of filing deadlines, one can make year-end adjustments with confidence. The calendar is not just a ledger of obligations but a map of possibilities, enabling better pricing, smarter purchasing, and well-timed investments.

Of course, there is a tension. Too rigid a calendar, enforced like dogma, risks suffocating adaptability. Life and business are both messy, and not every week or month will go as planned. The durable calendar is not a straightjacket but a spine: it supports flexibility without collapsing into chaos. It anchors the essential so that the optional can be navigated freely. Its strength lies in durability—not in capturing every fleeting task but in holding fast to the immovable ones.

In this light, the calendar is less a clerical tool and more a philosophy of attention. It embodies the belief that clarity, rhythm, and foresight are worth more than the thrill of improvisation. It recognises that keeping more of what you earn is not achieved through a single heroic decision but through a hundred small, pre-committed acts, spread across the cadence of a year.

The unresolved question remains: why do so many resist such a simple device, preferring instead to stumble into the same anxieties each year? Perhaps because clarity feels exposing; it leaves no excuse when discipline fails. Perhaps because the drama of last-minute survival appeals more to our egos than the quiet dignity of preparation. Yet the durable calendar asks us to choose: do we want the story of our financial year to be one of firefighting, or one of foresight? The answer, written on a single page, may determine not only how much we keep but how well we live.

Chapter 13
From Panic to Policy

The letter arrived on a Tuesday. A slim, innocuous envelope, no thicker than a phone bill, yet it carried a weight that emptied the stomach. A notice of penalty: late filing, interest compounded, and a threat of further action if ignored. The business owner had not intended negligence—he had been busy chasing clients, paying staff, juggling the thousand urgencies of keeping the lights on. But intent did not matter; the tax authority had its own clock, and he had slipped. In that moment, the enterprise he had poured years into was reduced to a number, a fine, a blot on a ledger. Panic set in.

Stories like this are not rare—they are the silent biographies of countless entrepreneurs, professionals, and even diligent employees who discover too late that financial fluency is not simply about earning but about rules, rhythms, and responses. The paradox is brutal: the same individuals who can negotiate complex contracts or deliver world-class work freeze at the sight of a tax notice. What they lack is not intelligence but policy—a set of rules so ingrained that panic has no oxygen.

Policy, in this sense, is not bureaucracy. It is personal lawmaking: *three rules you live by, without exception*. Always do. Never do. Review quarterly. These rules are the scaffolding that replaces frantic improvisation with calm execution. They shift the posture from reactive to proactive, from guilt-ridden delay to confident clarity. They do not eliminate complexity, but they contain it, keeping the human at the centre of the process rather than drowning in it.

The transition from panic to policy is the story of maturity. Early mistakes—missed deadlines, forgotten receipts, casual assumptions—are not merely administrative errors but symptoms of a deeper absence: the lack of codified principles. Just as nations stabilise by enacting constitutions, individuals stabilise by drafting their own rules. And unlike the dense legislation of governments, these personal tax constitutions must fit on a single page, or even a single breath.

Consider the owner who resolves: *Always set aside a percentage of every payment received. Never mix personal and business accounts. Review cash flow and obligations every quarter with a written note.* These three commitments, modest in wording, dismantle the recurring cycle of penalties and stress. They are not inspired by theory alone but by the lived recognition that behaviour, not intention, secures financial peace.

The significance runs deeper than administration. To move from panic to policy is to reclaim agency. Panic is the condition of being acted upon—by deadlines, by notices, by other people's timetables. Policy, by contrast, is the condition of acting upon oneself—of choosing in advance, of setting guardrails that hold firm even when attention falters. This is not simply about keeping more of what one earns but about preserving dignity and focus, about ensuring that time is spent on building, not firefighting.

The chapter ahead traces this path. It acknowledges the sting of fines and the shame of disorganisation, not as private failures but as common rites of passage. It then maps the progression towards fluency: how to write personal rules, how to anchor them in daily practice, and how to treat each quarter as a checkpoint for alignment. Along the way, it shows that clarity is less about knowing every regulation and more about knowing *your own non-negotiables.*

The unresolved question, one each reader must confront, is deceptively simple: if you had to write down three tax rules to govern your behaviour—rules so fundamental that they would withstand fatigue, distraction, and temptation—what would they be? To ask the question is to begin leaving panic behind. To answer it is to step into policy. The rest of this chapter is an invitation to do just that.

Write your three rules: Readers draft three personal tax policies—always do, never do, review quarterly—grounding behaviour beyond the book. A narrative shows the path from fines to fluency.

A solicitor once told of the moment she realised her legal expertise offered no shield against administrative neglect. After winning a complex case for a client, she celebrated with her team, only to return to her office and find a letter from the tax authority waiting on her desk. It was a penalty notice—interest and fines for late payment of a relatively minor obligation. She could recite statutes from memory, yet her own finances were compromised by something as simple as failing to check the calendar. The irony stung. What she lacked was not competence but discipline, and discipline in this arena is written down as rules.

The paradox is stark: highly intelligent, capable people—those who can navigate negotiations, build companies, or publish research of value—often stumble on basic tax administration. The reason is rarely ignorance of the law in detail. It is the absence of personal policy: a framework so clear and lived that it pre-empts panic. Without it, behaviour is dictated by circumstance—emails get buried, deadlines sneak past, stress accumulates. With it, clarity governs action long before urgency intrudes.

The concept of *three rules* is deliberately minimalist. It mirrors the principle of constitutions: brevity makes for longevity. A nation's founding document succeeds not by predicting every scenario but by distilling a few guardrails that endure. Likewise, the individual who sets three unwavering policies—an *always do*, a *never do*, and a *review quarterly*—lays down anchors that stabilise turbulent waters. More than any checklist, more than any detailed manual, these rules translate complexity into behaviour.

Take the first: *Always do.* This is the non-negotiable action that prevents drift. For some, it is the automatic set-aside—say 20% of every invoice into a separate account, untouchable until tax is due. For others, it is the routine reconciliation of bank feeds once a week. The action itself matters, less than the principle: something always done, no exceptions, no improvisation. The habit converts discipline from effort into default.

Then the second: *Never do.* This is the rule of prevention, the red line that shields against false economies and messy entanglements. A founder might write, *never pay business expenses from a personal card.* A consultant might insist, *never let a quarter close without invoicing outstanding work.* These rules feel narrow, but they guard against cascading problems—the late-night scramble to reconstruct records, the erosion of credibility when accounts are muddied, the unnecessary cost of professional clean-ups. A clear *never* is a shield against regret.

Finally, the *review quarterly*. Reflection is the most neglected tax skill. The pattern is familiar: one lives month to month, focused on delivery and growth, until the year ends and the reckoning arrives. By then, options are closed. Quarterly review breaks this trap. It is not the same as constant monitoring, which leads to fatigue. It is a rhythm, a scheduled pause every three months to ask: *Are the rules being kept? Do margins cover tax set-asides? Are there shifts in law or in life that require adjustment?* This cycle transforms tax from a once-a-year ambush into a steady, navigable current.

The effect of these three rules is not abstract. They map the journey from fines to fluency. Consider the small business owner who once dreaded tax season because every January brought chaos. After adopting his rules—*always reconcile weekly, never mix accounts, review quarterly with an accountant*—his experience changed within a year. There were no surprises, only adjustments. The fines disappeared, and with them the fear. He no longer waited for letters with a knot in his stomach. He had policy.

Critics might argue that three rules are too simplistic for a system as intricate as taxation. But the point is not to capture every nuance; it is to govern behaviour. Complexity is managed by professionals, by software, by detailed checklists. Simplicity is what governs in the midst of distraction. A surgeon does not memorise every surgical manual before entering the theatre; she relies on distilled checklists and core principles. Likewise, the taxpayer who internalises three rules is more prepared than one who memorises endless regulations but lacks behavioural anchors.

There is also a deeper philosophical resonance. Panic is reactive—it belongs to those who live under external control, always waiting for the next blow. Policy is proactive—it belongs to those who set their own boundaries and, by doing so, reclaim agency. To write down one's *always do, never do, review quarterly* is to assert that financial life is not an endless negotiation with bureaucracy but a domain where personal governance can prevail.

Drafting these rules demands thought. They cannot be copied wholesale from others, for what guards one business may not guard another. The owner of a consultancy may choose rules that prioritise timely invoicing and cash reserves. The restaurateur may write rules focused on stock write-offs and payroll compliance. The academic freelancer may focus on separating grants, stipends, and royalties. Each context dictates its own essentials, yet the structure—three rules only—forces clarity.

The exercise is deceptively powerful. When asked to define three rules, most people reach for five, ten, even twenty. They want to cover every angle. But the discipline of reducing to three exposes priorities. What truly matters? What habits would eliminate 80% of stress? The act of distillation itself sharpens judgment.

Imagine a room of entrepreneurs each reading aloud their three rules. The differences would be striking, but the commonalities would be profound: protect cash, prevent chaos, preserve rhythm. These are not merely administrative goals but markers of stewardship. They signal that money is no longer a source of anxiety but a resource governed with intent.

The unresolved challenge is not whether to write these rules but whether to live them. Will the set-aside account truly remain untouched? Will the quarterly review be honoured when deadlines pile up elsewhere? Policy without practice is a parchment constitution—it looks noble but collapses under stress. The test is in repetition, in habit, in resilience.

The next step, then, is not intellectual but practical. Take a page and write three rules: one *always do*, one *never do*, one *review quarterly*. They should be yours, not borrowed, short enough to remember, strong enough to hold. Once written, they will stand as a quiet constitution for your financial life. The question that lingers is this: in a year's time, when notices arrive for others but not for you, will you recognise that the difference lay not in luck or intelligence but in three sentences you chose to live by?

About the Author

Nicolette Sharma writes for people who build their own safety net. Raised between a shop floor and a kitchen table where bills were tallied by hand, she learned early that money is a story of rhythms, not windfalls. Her work blends plainspoken arithmetic with a historian's eye for why our systems look the way they do—from Kautilya's Arthashastra to the birth of VAT and pay-as-you-go. She believes good tax habits are civic, not just clever: separate the accounts, tell the truth in your records, and keep a small, steady calendar. When she's not simplifying rules for first-time founders and freelancers, she's walking city markets, noticing how prices, receipts, and human trust still fit together.

www.ingramcontent.com/pod-product-compliance
Lightning Source LLC
Chambersburg PA
CBHW031349230926
51848CB00002B/450
9789374121221